The *Selfish Capitalist*

To Jeremy Phillips and Ivan Ward,
founder members of the BioPsychoSocial Society, 1983

The Selfish Capitalist

Origins of Affluenza **Oliver James**

Vermilion
LONDON

1 3 5 7 9 10 8 6 4 2

Published in 2008 by Vermilion, an imprint of Ebury Publishing
A Random House Group Company

The Random House Group Limited Reg. No. 954009

Addresses for companies within the Random House Group
can be found at www.randomhouse.co.uk

A CIP catalogue record for this book is available from the British Library

The Random House Group Limited supports The Forest Stewardship
Council (FSC), the leading international forest certification organisation.
All our titles that are printed on Greenpeace approved FSC certified
paper carry the FSC logo. Our paper procurement policy
can be found at www.rbooks.co.uk/environment

Mixed Sources
Product group from well-managed
forests and other controlled sources
www.fsc.org Cert no. TT-COC-2139
© 1996 Forest Stewardship Council

Printed and bound in Great Britain by Mackays of Chatham PLC

Typeset by seagulls.net

HB ISBN 9780091923815
PB ISBN 9780091923860

To buy books by your favourite authors and register for offers visit
www.rbooks.co.uk

Contents

Introduction

There are enormous differences between nations in the amount that their citizens suffer emotional distress. In particular, based on the best available scientific evidence from the World Health Organization, twice as many people suffer in English-speaking nations compared with citizens of mainland Western European ones (23 per cent versus 11.5 per cent). To put it the other way round, on average, if you are a mainland Western European (from Germany, France, Holland, Belgium, Italy or Spain) you are half as likely to be suffering distress than if you are an American, British, Australian, Canadian or a New Zealander. What explains this huge difference, and what is the implication for how we organise our societies and lead our lives?

It was mainly in the introduction to my last book, *Affluenza*, that I sketched out some answers to these questions.

Nearly all of the subsequent chapters were limited to individual illustrations, and to personal and political solutions. In this book, I provide much more scientific detail regarding the causes of the difference between English-speaking and European nations, unfolded in a more systematic fashion, and I largely ignore the matter of solutions. But I also take the argument forward with two principal new sets of facts, neither uncontroversial and both easily dismissed as mere political ideology.

In the 1970s, the wealth of the richest people in the English-speaking world had been decreasing for several decades. A politico-economic creed which I term Selfish Capitalism (akin to Thatcherite or Reaganite neo-conservatism) emerged and was widely adopted. Its avowed object was to benefit everyone by increasing wealth. But it is a fact that one of its most significant consequences was to make the rich richer, whilst the average citizen's income did not increase at all after the 1970s. In every nation where Selfish Capitalism was introduced, the real wages of the majority either decreased or remained static. What was more, in many important respects, working conditions for ordinary people became considerably worse than they had been in the 1970s. Job security decreased dramatically (shorter contracts, less protection for employees) and for many, hours of work increased. The only reasons why average household affluence rose during this time was the increase in the proportion of women in the workforce and the longer hours worked.

The (often sincerely meant) rhetoric of Selfish Capitalism was that it would bring greater material opportunity for citizens and greater national wealth, enhancing well-being for all. In fact, while there was a *trickle up* effect for wealth and incomes, none of the much-heralded trickle down occurred. Whilst national wealth did increase, a very large proportion of it passed to the ruling elites, restoring them to a seemingly impregnable position of affluence not seen for forty years. Put bluntly, whether talking of Thatcherism, Reaganomics or Blairism, it enabled the rich to get richer. Demonstrating this, and the mechanisms by which it occurred, is the first new step taken here beyond those already made in *Affluenza*.

The second fact substantiated by this book is that the advent of Selfish Capitalism in English-speaking nations since the 1970s has caused a high increase in the amount of emotional distress (what psychiatrists call 'mental illness'), over and above any increasing trend since the 1950s. As far as I know, this assertion has not been made before, let alone supported by scientific evidence. Whilst distress may (or may not) have already been growing since the 1950s, the new contention here is that it grew more rapidly in the last thirty years.

To be absolutely clear, my new assertions are that

Selfish Capitalism led to a massive increase in the wealth of the wealthy, with no rise in average wages

and

there has been a substantial increase in emotional distress since the 1970s.

These assertions are not in themselves political, they are either true or false. Chapter 3 presents the evidence for them.

The cause of these changes is presented as being Selfish Capitalism and this, of course, is not a fact but a theory. Again, I would stress that I am not a member of any political party, that my primary motivation in advancing this theory is scholarly, not political. Nonetheless, the political and personal implications are considerable. By creating massive inequalities and insecure working conditions, and by wreaking havoc with our domestic lives, we became much more likely to be distressed. As in *Affluenza*, I maintain that the key factor in making these developments damaging was materialism (the technical word for what I termed the Affluenza Virus): placing too high a value on money, possessions, appearances and fame. My argument is that Selfish Capitalism increases materialism in developed nations, and since materialism causes emotional distress, Selfish Capitalism has caused a massive increase in the amount of emotional distress in the English-speaking nations.

If my Selfish Capitalism theory is debatable, so is a third new contention which I make. In chapter 4 I argue that the rise in geneticism, in general, and of evolutionary psychology, in particular, have been highly significant as ideologies in gaining support for Selfish Capitalism. Since the 1970s there has been a resurgence of the view that the difference between you and your siblings is much influenced by differences in your genes. It has also become fashionable to believe that our fundamental purpose is to reproduce our selfish genes. Everything about our psychology – be it gender differences, homosexuality or emotional distress – is said to be ultimately traceable back to a genetically encoded adaptation to condi-tions many thousands of years ago. My new contention is that the peddling and acceptance of this geneticism and evolutionary psychology have been important factors in making the general population susceptible to the idea that Selfish Capitalism will be good for them. Selfish Gene-ery and Selfish Capitalism make very comfortable intellectual bedfellows. That we are machines for genetic replication justifies boundless greed, in some minds. That genes explain our behaviour and well-being distracts attention from society as a cause; such ideas also encourage us to accept or pursue chemical, physical solutions, not social change.

Furthermore, I question the basis of the 'science' on which the burgeoning geneticism and evolutionary theory is based and propose that instead, we should focus on the principal causes of emotional distress in English-speaking developed nations: early childhood maltreatment and Selfish Capitalism. That we would have half as much emotional distress if we were Unselfish Capitalist, like mainland Western Europe, strikes me as far more significant than speculation of what may have gone on thousands of years ago during our evolution.

I begin with my view of the fundamental causes of emotional distress (chapter 1). This has to be where any explanation of differences in rates between nations would start: the factors that could explain such differences. I dismiss genes as being unlikely to play any significant part but there are many other competitors for attention, from parental care to social class to urbanicity. I do my best to explain, briefly, how each of these impact at different levels.

Having zeroed in on the specific question of differences in amounts of distress between contemporary developed nations, I propose materialism as being critical. Chapter 2 provides the full scientific evidence for its role. Materialists have been shown to be more likely to be distressed than non-materialists, and there are a number of reasons why it has this effect. Materialists are more emotionally insecure, have poorer quality personal relationships, are more inauthentic and lacking in a sense of autonomy, and have lower self-esteem. They watch more television, and the kind of programmes they tend to prefer make them more materialistic. As children they are likely to have parents who make love conditional on performance and are obsessed with results at school, making their offspring materialistic.

Chapter 3 defines what I mean by Selfish Capitalism, distinguishing it from close relatives, like Thatcherism, neo-liberalism and Free Market Economics. To illustrate how it affects societies, I examine changes in two societies after they adopted Selfish Capitalism at the end of the 1970s, the USA and UK. As already noted, they became more unequal and working conditions became more insecure. But a set of harmful and related further changes occurred. Consumerism increased, personal savings collapsed, property prices spiralled and above all, personal life was colonised by work. In terms of our levels of distress, increased materialism is presented as a key factor and two tests are offered of the Selfish Capitalist theory of emotional distress: new evidence is provided demonstrating that there has been a sharp increase in distress since the 1970s in English-speaking nations, following their adoption of Selfish Capitalist governance; and, further evidence shows that citizens of Selfish Capitalist, English-speaking nations are much more distressed than those of (Unselfish Capitalist) mainland Western Europe.

Chapter 4 completes the argument, presenting an analysis of how Selfish Capitalism reproduces itself. I contend that geneticism and evolutionary psychology played a significant role in encouraging citizens of English-speaking nations to accept Selfish Capitalist governance. In addition, I speculate that a variety of social trends were encouraged by Selfish Capitalism to help it thrive, from the rise in positive psychology and Cognitive Behavioural Therapy (CBT), to the pressure for both parents to do paid work when their children are small.

Above all, my conclusion is that Selfish Capitalism actively encourages distress, feasting upon it. I maintain that there is a simple solution for English-speaking nations: become Unselfish Capitalist. It is incumbent on our politicians to heed this message and to begin the long journey back towards societies which put well-being before the wealth of a tiny minority.

Before beginning, there are a few pieces of intellectual housekeeping required regarding the terms I am using.

When writing of materialism, for most of the book I am referring to what I term the 'relative' rather than the 'survival' variety. A person who is desperate for money because they are starving, homeless or in urgent need of medical assistance is engaged in survival materialism: it entails the meeting of a fundamental human need. Such materialism is not a cause of distress. For example, the average Eastern European worker who has come to the UK because of the five- or six-fold higher hourly rate of pay is doing so in order to be able to save enough money to buy a new home back in their country of birth. This is a need, not a want, because as a result of Selfish Capitalisation of Eastern Europe, state provision of housing has declined and there is great pressure to find capital sums in order to avoid living in squalor.

By contrast, a person whose fundamental practical needs are met, as is the case for most of the citizens in the developed world, but who is still highly materialistic, is engaged in relative materialism: in essence, they want the money, possessions, appearances or fame in order to keep up with the Joneses. It is these people who are placed at greater risk of distress by their materialism, like the many examples I provided in *Affluenza*. Thus, for the most part, this book concerns the materialism of people in developed rather than developing nations: the focus is relative materialism.

When writing of emotional distress, I have eschewed the term mental illness for the simple reason that, as explained in *Affluenza*, I do not consider the vast majority of mental and emotional states which are categorised as illnesses by psychiatrists (doctors) to be best conceived as physical pathologies. Rather, as is made clear in chapter 1, they are psychological responses to a variety of unpleasant environ- mental influences. The specific ill-being that I mean by emotional distress is depression, anxiety, substance abuse and impulse disorder (like quick-temperedness, impulsivity), basing this on the definitions used in the WHO study.

Finally, this book is not about happiness, life satisfaction or quality of life, terms that have been given widespread attention in recent years by politicians, some authors and many newspapers. As also detailed in *Affluenza*, I do not consider the measurement of these states to be based on convincing scientific methods but here, I go further. The enthusiastic adoption of the fantasy of happiness as a lure for electors and of sticking-plaster psychologies, like CBT, by Selfish Capitalism has been a major distraction from the real problem: the epidemic of emotional distress which this book seeks to explain.

Chapter 1
The Fundamental Causes of Emotional Distress

Why does emotional distress exist?

The modern vogue is to seek out evolutionary purposes for emotional distress. Because the theory of natural selection proposes that only those traits that have served an adaptive purpose survive, everything about us must have been adaptive at some point in our evolution (even if it no longer is helpful and, in theory, dying out) to have remained in our gene pool. The corollary is that everything about us must also be ultimately traceable back to our genetic inheritance, even traits which on the face of it are extremely maladaptive. Evolutionists pay virtually no attention to the considerable number of traits which might seem to be solely maladaptive, in terms of helping to reproduce genes. One might ponder why Down's syndrome endures, why genetic abnormalities which guarantee extremely low intelligence continue, or even why homosexuality (if one assumes, as geneticists must do, that it has a genetic foundation) persists – whatever the other merits of this sexual orientation, reproduction is by definition not one of them. I am looking forward to the first evolutionary theory explaining why nuclear weapons or ecologically unsustainable economics, adaptations which may destroy all life on this planet, will further the reproduction of genes.

In the case of emotional distress, considerable imagination is required to find adaptive purposes. How can being trapped in your home by agoraphobia, or killing yourself, or claiming you are Jesus Christ, make it more likely that you will reproduce? Undaunted, the evolutionists have risen to the challenge. It has been argued that schizophrenia helped our species to think outside the box. Observation of monkeys suggests that depression-like, subordinate, low-status-indicating behaviour helps them to survive by reducing the risk of them being killed by higher-status members of the troop. In humans, the legacy is said to be the depressive trait of running oneself down, originating as a way of avoiding posing a threat to stronger people.

Less prosaically, the expression of distress in monkeys and other mammals serves some indisputably useful purposes. For the individual, screams or subdued behaviour encourage other members of the troop to come to their aid, and for the group they send out a warning of threats. In the same way, a baby's crying is an indication that something is troubling it, a signal to carers to take action. In later life, expressed distress serves the same purpose between adults, and is even, arguably, a way for people to warn themselves that something is wrong – if we shed tears, it not only tells others that we are in trouble, it brings it home to ourselves.

But this does not prove that these behaviours evolved as part of our genetic armoury. It is one thing to demonstrate that a behaviour has beneficial (or adverse) consequences, quite another to prove that this is its purpose, let alone that it has become part of our genes for this reason. Arguing from the results of phenomena back to causes is not a reliable scientific method. An artist may create works which sell at huge prices, but that does not prove that the reason for creating them was to get rich. Drunken drivers who cause injuries through dangerous driving did not usually become intoxicated for the purpose of injuring others. However fascinating and amusing (often unintentionally) evolutionary theories may be, they remain speculations, currently not amenable to scientific proof.

Personally, I have little doubt that genes confer upon us fundamental psychological potentials, such as anger, humour, sexual desire and social comparison. I daresay that one day, molecular geneticists will prove this but until then we have no other method for doing so.

To my mind, anyway, the key question does not concern human universals so much as the degree of their plasticity. The huge variety in people from different families and nations suggest it is considerable. Take language, for instance. Unless severely neglected in early life or biologically damaged, all humans develop language, suggesting that a genetic programme exists to acquire it. This may or may not have evolved along the lines proposed by Darwinists and neo-Darwinists, but far more significant, I believe, is what our environments do with that potentiality.

Which language we speak depends completely on which one we are exposed to. Our use of it is shaped by the national culture, for example whether we tend to use superlatives (USA) or understatement (New Zealand). Most significant of all, the vast variation in the use of a particular language between individuals from the same society depends on our family culture and the specifics of the care we received in our early years. For practical purposes, national and individual differences are far more important than the fact that language is conferred on us by genes. Likewise, it is plausible that the presence of emotional distress in our human repertoire reflects our evolution, but cross-national differences in rates of distress have little, if any, genetic cause.

When you survey the literature on the causes of emotional distress, it is abundantly clear that most cases, perhaps the vast majority of them, are responses to environmental factors. This is so whether you ask 'Why is there more emotional distress in some nations than in others?', or 'Why are some people within a given nation more prone to emotional distress than others?' or finally, 'Why are some offspring of the same parents more prone to emotional distress than others?' Even mainstream psychiatrists and psychologists accept that the environment plays a major role – factors such as being sexually abused as a child, being poor or being unemployed – but they maintain that genes affect how vulnerable we are to these adversities, explain why one person succumbs but not their sibling. Hardly any scientists dare say so in print, but I suspect that a fair few also believe that genetic differences between ethnic groups, social classes and nations affect vulnerability. These genetic influences may exist but, as I shall explain, there are strong reasons for doubting that they do.

Whilst of enduring fascination, the questions of why siblings have different vulnerabilities to distress and why some people from within a given nation are more at risk than others are less central to the main subject of this book than that of why nations differ. I shall take each in turn, but concentrate most of my attention on this latter.

Early childhood experience: why are some offspring of the same parents more prone to emotional distress than others?

Early Care

As described in my book *They F*** You Up*, my main answer is that siblings differ because they were treated differently during early childhood. Contrary to decades of claims that early experiences have no special influence on subsequent emotional well-being and personality, it is finally becoming apparent that negative experiences during the first five years do cause more damage than those in subsequent years. Many thousands of studies suggest this, and some of the most telling examples are described in this section.

In the case of sexual abuse, the earlier it occurs, the greater number of sub-personalities a survivor is likely to develop in later life and the more profound the damage to the sense of self. Likewise for physical abuse. In a sample of 578 children assessed in kindergarten and through into adolescence, those who were physically abused in the first five years of life were significantly more maladjusted in adolescence than those who were first abused after the age of five, or not at all. Similarly, the earlier a child became neglected, or had parents who divorced, separated or suffered financial misfortune, the greater the likelihood of later emotional distress. Amongst 800 children aged nine, the ones who had suffered severe maltreatment before the age of three were more disturbed than the ones who had been severely maltreated between the ages of three and five (but not aged nought to three), and they in turn were more disturbed than children who had only suffered it aged five to nine. Studies of adoptees suggest that the older the child when adopted, the greater the damage. Whilst intellectual deficits can often be largely reversed by stimulating adoptive environments, lasting psychopathology is found in significant proportions even where the adoptive nurture is first-rate. Causal links have been demonstrated between adult personality disorder and maltreatment before the age of two; one study has shown this to be the strongest single predictor of dissociation at age nineteen, after allowing for quality of subsequent care and other factors. On top of this, it now seems clear that psychoanalyst John Bowlby was essentially correct in his claim that the period from six months to three years is a sensitive time for forming a secure pattern of attachment. If patterns do subsequently change, this is rule-governed, according to predictable environmental factors such as adult divorce or bereavement. Many studies of animals have shown that early experience has a greater effect on the brain but it is only recently that evidence of this has been provided in humans. For example, lasting damage to cortisol levels and persistently atypical brainwave patterns have been demonstrated in children whose mothers were depressed when they were infants, regardless of whether the mother recovered from the depression. The very size of brain structures can be affected by early care: for example, the volume of the hippocampal region of the brain is 5 per cent less in women who were sexually abused as children. The earlier that abuse is suffered, the greater the reduction in intracranial volume. It is increasingly apparent that patterns of neurotransmitters and hormone levels are often an effect of past and present psychosocial processes, rather than of physiology or genetics. On average, a girl whose father divorces or separates from her mother and leaves the home before she is aged ten comes into puberty six months earlier than a girl from an intact family, and early pubescence is a strong correlate of sexual promiscuity and substance abuse. If fathers are physically present but the family is conflict-filled, their daughters come into puberty significantly earlier than those with close relationships.

This is not to say that we emerge on our sixth birthday fully formed, done and dusted. Subsequent experiences can also be very influential, in combination with the early ones. All of us are scripted roles in our family drama, cast as the clever or dim one, the outgoing or introverted, the amusing or serious. Our order in the family, combined with our gender, plays a big role in how we are cast, and so does the baggage our parents bring to their task. What is more, major life events, such as the death of a parent or their divorce, can still change our trajectory very significantly, from the age of six.

Genes

Many readers will find it implausible that differences in early childhood care could play such an important role in making siblings different from one another. Surely genes must play some role? Well, I daresay they do, but at present the evidence for this is slight and questionable. It has become commonplace to assert that, in general, one half of the difference between individual siblings is attributable to genes. This 'bit of both' idea seems cosily commonsensical, and is attractive as a way of avoiding tedious nature-versus-nurture disputation. Yet if we accept widely cited surveys of results of twins studies, although the point is never spelt out, they simply do not support the 'bit of both' theory. Only a handful of all the aspects of human psychology exceed 50 per cent heritability, however selectively you sift through the studies. In the case of emotional distress, heritability does reach 50 per cent in the rare and extreme cases of autism, schizophrenia, manic depression and major depression. But this should not distract from the overall fact that genes play only a small role in causing the vast majority of emotional distress – minor depression and neurosis, which are 30 per cent heritable at most. Furthermore, if twin studies are to be believed, genes play little or no role at all in causing individual differences in many important behaviours (eg attachment patterns, heterosexual attraction preferences and violence). Despite dozens of false dawns, molecular genetics has still to identify replicated genetic loci for a single emotional distress, unless you include Huntington's and familial Alzheimer's diseases.

The most promising example of molecular genetic research concerns what is known as the serotonin transponder gene. Very recently, as a result of the Human

Genome Project, a New Zealand study headed by Absalom Caspi found that certain genetic variations created the vulnerability to depression, cannabis use and violence. If you had the wrong genes, good early care meant they were not likely to find expression in dysfunction but bad care meant you developed those problems in later life; likewise, if you did not have those genes, even if you had bad care you were much less likely to develop the problems. This greatly accords with the 'bit of both' model. However, the jury is very much out on the role of this gene. On the one hand, four studies have partially replicated the original finding of the effect of the gene on depression. Unfortunately, all these studies had small samples, categorised the gene in different ways and in two of them, the replication was only for women, not men. Three other small studies also provide partial support for the gene's role. All of this evidence is widely accepted to be very far from conclusive as replication of Caspi's original findings. Furthermore, three further studies have not replicated the effect of the gene on depression – possession of it did not result in depression. One of these studies had a much larger sample than all the replication studies, and in this case, people with the genetic variation which should have made them vulnerable to depression in the event of adverse early care were actually less vulnerable, an important contradiction of the original study. Furthermore, in large studies of samples of depressed patients, their genes do not vary in the predicted manner compared with undepressed people: the depressed are not more likely to have the variant which increased the likelihood of depression when coupled with childhood maltreatment.

On a wider scale, there are reasons to question the role of this genetic variation. Two of the strongest predictors of who gets depressed in a developed nation are being of low income and being a woman – the poor and females are twice as likely as the rich and males to be depressed. Two studies have found no greater occurrence of the supposedly depression-inducing genetic variation in low-income people. What is more, in all but two of the replication studies mentioned above, the gene is not found more often in women than men. At best, the implication of this line of research so far is that the genetic variation may play no part in causing depression and even if it does turn out to play a role, the key factor is whether the environment is adverse – especially, whether there has been childhood maltreatrment.

Similar studies of Attention Deficit Hyperactivity Disorder have also been done, with mixed outcomes. In the coming years, it is possible that other studies will show that we are born with potentials for all kinds of problems which are only fulfilled if our parenting is poor but as yet, this has not been proven and may never be.

Indeed, so recalcitrant have the genes identified by the Human Genome Project been in offering any evidence, the principal researchers now all accept that there are no single 'genes for' emotional distresses. The fallback position is that many combinations of genes, rather than single ones, must be responsible, but this remains to be established. That leaves twin studies as the principal source of evidence – and there are well-founded reasons to question them. For one thing, adoption studies consistently demonstrate substantially lower estimates of heritability than twin studies. For another, there are fundamental problems with the twins method that are rarely even referred to, even though they could mean that heritability estimates based on it are worthless. Indeed, responding to the unexpectedly small number of genes identified by the Human Genome Project, one of its principal scientists has cast serious doubt on the likelihood that genes play much role in causing individual differences at all.

The social implications of early experience having such a major impact on how we turn out are momentous. They are an imperative for governments to create societies which maximise the likelihood of parents meeting their small children's needs. They also feed into the answer provided to my further questions.

Differences within nations: why are some individuals within a given society more prone to emotional distress than others?

Within developed nations, the combination of a person's social class, gender, age, ethnicity and place of residence (urban versus rural) strongly predict whether they will become emotionally distressed. Someone from the lowest class is about twice as likely to suffer the commonest problems, such as depression and anxiety, as someone from the highest one. Correlating with this, the more academic qualifications people have, the less emotionally distressed they are, partly because the rich also tend to be well educated. Women in most societies are about twice as likely to suffer depression and anxiety as men, poor women up to nine times more so than rich men, mothers with small children more so than women whose children are grown up. Men are at greater risk of alcoholism and other substance abuses than women. The young suffer all the common emotional distresses more than the old, sixteen- to twenty-four-year-olds being at much greater risk than over-sixties. Immigrant populations are at greater risk than indigenous ones: for example, rates of schizophrenia amongst British Afro– Caribbeans are dramatically higher, about nine times more than indigenous Caucasians. Finally, urban dwellers are about twice as much more likely to suffer than the rural.

The explanation for the impact of these factors is that each one piles on stressors. Those on a low income or unemployed face the real danger of eviction for not being able to pay the rent, and the absence of money as a means for dealing with the short-term daily hassles of everyday life, from the advantages of having a car to visit the supermarket, to the convenience of being able to afford babysitters, to the luxury of being able to afford e-number-free food which will not make your children hyperactive. The travails of post-feminist modern womanhood are many and irksome, from the role strain created by motherhood and careers, to the pressure to look like Maria Sharapova. Likewise, the difficulties of the young have been massively compounded by the rise of individualism and the pressure to compare their performance with that of others in an ever-widening number of domains (sexual performance, personality, possessions). The massive strains put on immigrant communities extend far beyond the casual racism that still greets them, from the problem of acquiring a new language, to uncertainties about their legal status, to separation from friends and family in their country of origin. Finally, whilst country life may never have been bucolic, it still has the great advantage of not being accompanied by as much petty crime and violence, or a frantic pace of life and heavy pollution.

Not all of the impact of being in one of these social categories is attributable to the contemporary pressures thereof. Patterns of nurture in early life differ between classes, for example, as well as between genders and for different generations. These patterns interact with the social categories. Hence, being a low-income, relatively uneducated mother, without the help that money can buy, makes you more likely to be irritable and to hit your children as a way of disciplining them, putting them at greater risk of both depression and aggression. Similarly, being a fifteen-year-old girl from a high social class makes you far more likely to have been subjected to over-controlling, perfectionist mothering, also increasing your risk. Patterns of nurture thus both explain and are explained by contemporary pressures. What is more, not all low-income or female or young people suffer from emotional distresses when subjected to the pressures of their social category. Differences in early childhood experience within a class or gender play a major role in increasing or decreasing vulnerability to subsequent adversities.

In theory, genetic differences could also be playing a part, by influencing what categories people are in. By definition, genes determine gender, but as yet there is no evidence that women have genetic endowments that predispose them to greater emotional distress. The fact that women's increased risk disappears in Denmark, Finland and Norway, or amongst the Amish in the USA, or amongst Jewish Englishwomen, suggests that differing gender roles and nurture of women are critical. Low-income people could be in that position because of genes, as was famously argued by Richard Herrnstein and Charles Murray in their book *The Bell Curve*. Low intelligence, greater vulnerability to emotional distress, defective character – all could be inherited and make it more likely that a person will sink to join the 'sludge' at the bottom of the gene pool. But again, it does not seem to be so. Studies show that, on average, a person from a poor home who is adopted at birth into a middle-class home has an IQ score ten points higher than their biological parents. At the very least, this suggests that the rearing environment can make a significant difference to intelligence.

As for emotional distress, studies of levels of serotonin (a neurotransmitter, reduced levels of which are associated with depression) show that low classes are more likely to have low levels. However, other studies reveal that low-income people are no more likely than high-income ones to have mutations of the gene which is thought to be important in the manufacture of serotonin. The notion that youth in itself, through genes, causes emotional distress is easily dismissed – it is only recently and only in some nations that youth in itself has become a predictor of distress. Regarding ethnicity, in the case of Afro–Caribbeans, the rates of schizophrenia amongst those who stayed in the homeland compared with rates amongst their relatives who emigrated to Britain are far lower, the same as those found in the rest of the home population. Finally, there is considerable evidence that city-dwellers are not a genetically vulnerable group drawn by the lure of the bright lights – it is not the case that cities attract people who are more vulnerable to distress as a result of genes, than people who stay in the countryside.

Differences between nations: why is there more emotional distress in some nations than in others?

Although there have been several hundred surveys of rates of emotional distress in countries around the world (200 of them in Europe since 1980), for all sorts of reasons, the results are mostly not much use for making comparisons between nations. Most of the samples studied were not representative of the whole nation in which they were done. Different instruments for measuring rates produce different results, so that the results of ones which assess rates of psychological distress (so-called 'minor' emotional distresses, eg minor depression or anxiety), such as the General Health Questionnaire, are different from those based on the psychiatric bible (the DSM – *Diagnostic and Statistical Manual of Mental Disorders*). Comparison can be safely made only between studies in different nations which used the same instruments, in the same way. Results also differ between questionnaires filled out by subjects and those resulting from face-to-face interviews. With interview-based surveys, trained psychiatrists get different results from lay interviewers, even if the latter have been especially trained. Finally, the precise meaning of the words used in the questions that are asked may differ between nations, and there are very different levels of awareness in different nations of the issues about which subjects are being questioned. For example, the Chinese conceptualise questions about mental states differently from Westerners, and tend to talk about what we would regard as bodily states when asked about their emotions.

To overcome these obstacles, a worldwide study of twenty-five nations by the World Health Organization is

Prevalence of Emotional Distress in Fifteen Countries (emotional distress measured: depression, anxiety, substance abuse and impulse disorders).

Nation	Percentage of population having suffered a mental distress in the last 12 months
USA	26.4
New Zealand	20.7
Ukraine	20.5
France	18.4
Colombia	17.8
Lebanon	16.9
Netherlands	14.9
Mexico	12.2
Belgium	12.0
Spain	9.2
Germany	9.1
China (Beijing)	9.1
Japan	8.8
Italy	8.2
Nigeria	4.7
China (Shanghai)	4.3

under way, using the same methods everywhere, with properly representative samples and great effort put into making the questions as culture-neutral as possible. The results are as reliable an indicator of the international distribution of emotional distress as exists. The results for the fifteen countries for which results have so far been published are given in the table opposite. The USA has, by some margin, the largest prevalence: over a quarter of Americans had been distressed in the previous twelve months, around six times the levels found in Shanghai (4.3 per cent) and Nigeria (4.7 per cent).

In considering the causes of these large differences, there is overwhelming evidence that genes can be ruled out. In the first place, it is very unlikely that there is any significant difference between the gene pool of Caucasian Americans and the Europeans from whom they are mostly descended, yet the prevalences of distress are very different. For example, Italian–Americans seem to have prevalences three times higher than the descendants of Italians who remained in Europe. Likewise, African–Americans of Nigerian origin would appear to have rates six times higher than Nigerians whose ancestors were not taken as slaves and remained in Africa. It is conceivable that the Italians who emigrated had genes which predisposed them to move country, and that they also overlap with genes for higher rates of distress. Conceivable, though highly improbable, is that the Nigerians who were enslaved had genes that made them more vulnerable to being captured which overlap with distress genes. Neither of these seem very likely and convincing evidence to the contrary comes from studies of voluntarily immigrant populations.

These studies demonstrate that when citizens of a nation emigrate to another one, within a few generations they begin to exhibit the distress rates of their adoptive nation. The more they develop the habits, attitudes and behaviour of their adoptive nation, the more precisely they duplicate that nation's rates. Thus, if a citizen of Nigeria moves to the USA and raises a family there, to the extent that they become American, their offspring or grandchildren will develop American rates. If national or ethnic differences in genes caused differences in susceptibility to emotional distress, then, over several generations, and taking levels of acculturation into account, immigrants should display different rates to host populations. But they do not usually do so, and where they do it is because they have not acculturated to their adoptive society rather than because of genes. Thus, in explaining international differences, it is to factors other than genes to which we must turn.

Socio-economic upheaval

This factor can be dealt with quickly. For self-evident reasons, civil wars and major economic disasters can explain why a country has a high rate. For example, Uganda has been riven by civil strife for many years. When a sample from one of the areas that had been strongly affected by these horrors was compared with another area that had not, the strife-afflicted area had rates of severe depression four times higher. A similar study done in Uganda in 1979 found the same. Social unrest and civil war may also help to explain the high rates of emotional distress found in Colombia and the Lebanon by the WHO study.

As for economic disaster, the countries of the former Soviet Union have suffered it on a large scale. Unfortunately there are no reliable studies from the Soviet era in those countries, but studies done since the introduction of market liberalism reveal high rates of emotional distress. In the WHO study results listed on page 32, Ukraine comes third in the league table of woe. A more recent study of depression in Russian, Polish and Czech cities found high rates (albeit using the kind of measurement instrument that generally obtains higher levels than obtained using the DSM). Amongst the women, depression was found in 44 per cent of the Russians, 40 per cent of the Poles and 34 per cent of the Czechs. Most scientists suspect that these high rates did not predate the huge turbulence of the economic crashes that each country has suffered, including mass unemployment and the loss of all savings.

Measuring rates in nations which have recently endured these calamities is not terribly revealing of national differences. If you measured rates in New York following the stock market crash of 1929 or in the USA generally during the Great Depression, the results would not be a reliable indication of emotional distress in the USA during less turbulent times. More interesting is when we consider more stable societies, unaffected by recent socio-economic earthquakes.

Industrialisation and urbanisation

Industrialisation and urbanisation are arguably the fundamental causes of high rates of emotional distress. As Emil Durkheim's famous study of suicide in nineteenth-century Europe suggested, the higher the proportion of a nation's population employed in factories and in the bureaucracies which invariably accompany them, the more emotional distress (although Durkheim's data have since been queried). Industrialisation usually coincides with a shift from rural to urban living, and the impact of the one is closely connected to the impact of the other: together and separately, they tend to cause a plethora of other emotional distress-inducing social changes. The transition from extended to nuclear families is often hastened, so that parents and grandparents are less likely to live near one another, relatives are dispersed to other locations, and neighbours are usually unrelated by blood. In hard times, the reciprocity that characterises rural life is no longer there as a safety-net, and in the absence of state-provided welfare, theft and robbery become common responses to hardship. The relationships of parents with their children become more unstable, and rates of divorce and separation increase. The loss of social cohesion, the social isolation and fractured relationships increase the likelihood of children being neglected or abused and of the elderly suffering the same. Individualism replaces collectivism, so that identity is achieved through performance at school and through career, rather than conferred by social class, background, family roles and gender. Education of younger generations divides them from older ones, to whom they are less respectful or obedient. Religious observance decreases, with morality no longer founded on belief in a divinely ordained ethos and with a loss of community from dwindling church attendance.

The clearest evidence that industrialisation causes emotional distress, compared with life in settled, pre-industrial agrarian communities, comes from international studies of schizophrenia, a form of distress which has been found everywhere that it has been studied. Schizophrenia is often held to be of largely genetic origin, yet it is much less common in pre-industrial peasant communities than in industrialised or industrialising communities, only a quarter as common in the case of some variants of the illness. There is also a far greater likelihood of recovery in such societies and a far smaller likelihood of recurrence. The direct causal role of urban living in schizophrenia has been recently demonstrated. Urban dwellers are more likely to suffer it, and the likelihood increases in direct proportion to the time spent living in the city before becoming distressed. The risk of developing schizophrenia as a result of urban life is four times greater than the risk created by having had an afflicted mother. Some have countered that there is a tendency for vulnerable people to drift towards city living, but this has been shown to be false. Rather, factors of city life such as stressful life events (eg rape or homelessness), isolation and pressures peculiar to urban poverty, such as high rates of drug abuse, have been shown to be crucial.

A similar story emerges from international studies of depression. A recent example compared depression in rural and urban settings in Nigeria and the USA. In both countries it was much commoner in the urban groups. Likewise, a meta-survey found significantly more depression amongst urban than amongst rural Europeans, in Britain nearly twice as much. The urbanites were more stressed about housing, work, marriage, child-rearing and personal safety, as well as feeling more isolated and disconnected from their community.

Studies of the impact of consumerism on developing nations, an important by-product of industrialisation and a correlate of materialism, suggest that it reduces well-being. Such societies rapidly become more unequal, inter-class tensions increase, and with the arrival of the consumer frustration and resulting stress that we now all take for granted (battling with call centres, constantly having to change mortgage providers) come higher rates of emotional distress.

In summarising the evidence of the ill-being that accompanies industrialisation, Arthur Kleinman estimated that three-quarters of the hundreds of diseases listed in the DSM are found almost exclusively in the USA and in Westernised elites, whether Asian or European. Problems such as multiple personality disorder, eating disorders and chronic fatigue syndrome are very largely caused by industrialisation and are virtually unknown in pre-industrial communities.

If one accepts this reading of the evidence – and not all experts in the field do – then industrialisation would seem to exact a very large toll in exchange for the material benefits it supplies. We may be a whole lot better fed, housed, transported, medically treated, and so on, but industrialised nations are probably many times more prone to emotional distress than any others in the history of the world. Depending on which study you believe, an American today is between three and ten times more likely to suffer from depression than in 1950, and there are similar findings for other developed nations (Sweden, New Zealand, Germany and Canada). If studies existed of rates of distress four hundred years ago, there are strong grounds for supposing that those rates would be considerably lower than in the developed world in 1950. But the principal argument of this book is that the problem does not end with industrialisation.

Differences in distress across the developed world

In the results of the WHO study presented on page 32, socio-economic upheavals could largely explain the high prevalence found the Ukraine, Colombia and the Lebanon. Urbanisation and industrialisation have proceeded at varying paces and in different forms in these and the other developing nations in the study (Mexico, Nigeria and

China), possibly explaining some of the differences between these developing nations. But where developed like is compared directly with developed like, the results are intriguing. All have comparable levels of urbanisation and industrialisation, but none has suffered severe socio-economic upheavals in recent years.

The USA and New Zealand have a much higher prevalence of distress (an average of over 23 per cent). If you combine the results for the mainland Western European nations (France, the Netherlands, Belgium, Spain, Germany and Italy) and if you also add Japan, the average is 11.5 per cent. Although it is much more debatable, you can also add the results for national surveys of distress in the UK, Australia and Canada (see Appendix 2). Debatable, because these studies have not used identical instruments for measuring distress to those employed in the 2004 WHO study, they were not done in exactly the same year (though all were completed within two years of the WHO data-gathering) and did not employ exactly the same interviewing methods. With those reservations noted, however, it is also intriguing that when you combine the results for all the English-speaking nations from these surveys (USA, New Zealand, UK, Australia and Canada), the average is still 23 per cent. Taken overall, it is my contention that there is good reason, therefore, to suppose that English-speaking nations have twice the prevalence of mainland European ones. I further contend that the explanation is a cause of distress that I have not mentioned so far: materialism.

Chapter 2

Materialism: a Major Cause of Modern Distress

We have seen that emotional distress is caused at several different levels, from the familial, to social class or gender, to the national, with many factors involved. Until recently, the degree to which a person was materialistic – placing a high value on money, possessions, appearances and fame – was not even considered by the vast majority of students of the subject as playing any role in causing distress at any level. As I shall outline in the first part of this chapter, the theory that it might do was systematically laid out more than fifty years ago by an American psychologist, Erich Fromm, but scientific tests of materialism's role did not begin in earnest until the last fifteen. It is clear from these studies that materialism and distress go together: unmaterialistic people are less likely to suffer, highly materialistic, more likely. It will also emerge that materialism is a link in the chain of causation and has both familial and wider societal causes.

Hence, two siblings raised by the same parents may vary in how materialistic they are, depending on the particular way their parents relate to them. The children of families with similar incomes and social conditions living in the same street may also vary, depending on the values of the parents in each household. In the same way, nations vary in their level of materialism, depending on their histories, cultures and contemporary politics.

A vital distinction must be drawn at the outset between 'survival' and 'relative' materialism. People living in absolute poverty in developing nations are very liable to be materialistic, which is hardly surprising. Not knowing where their next meal will come from or how to afford basic medical care, they will be liable to see money and possessions as of huge importance, a matter of survival. Far from making them emotionally distressed, the achievement of these goals in even a small way will improve their wellbeing. But in developed nations, where basic material needs have been met – estimated to require an annual income of only £15,000 – and people are highly materialistic, this materialism is usually relative. I say 'usually', because in some developed nations, certain basic needs cannot be met even with that amount of money. In the USA, there are 43 million people without health insurance, putting them at considerable medical risk. Arguably, placing a high value on money by such people is survival materialism, so the precise point at which materialism become relative is not clear-cut. In essence, it depends on the degree to which the high premium placed on money, possessions, appearance or fame is in order to meet a fundamental psychological need, or if it is to keep up with the Joneses. Defined in this way, in the case of anyone who is materialistic and who has the income and wealth of a person in the top three-quarters of a developed nation, their materialism is relative. The research in what follows applies to such relatively affluent people. It shows that those with relative materialism are significantly more likely to be emotionally distressed than ones who are unmaterialistic. Henceforth, to avoid repetition, when I use the word 'materialism' I shall mean 'relative materialism', unless I specify otherwise.

As we shall see in succeeding chapters, this evidence greatly assists in explaining why English-speaking nations are twice as distressed as mainland European ones: materialism is a key factor.

Erich Fromm's theory of American consumerism

Erich Fromm provided much of the theoretical impetus for modern empirical studies of materialists. Whilst several other important thinkers from the Frankfurt School, such as Herbert Marcuse, thought along similar lines, Fromm is the most enduring influence. He described American society in 1955 thus: 'We have a literacy rate above 90 per cent of the population. We have radio, television, movies, a newspaper a day for everybody. But instead of giving us the best of past and present literature and music, these media of communication, supplemented by advertising, fill the minds of men with the cheapest trash, lacking any sense of reality, with sadistic phantasies which a halfway-cultured person would be embarassed to entertain even once in while. But while the mind of everybody, young and old, is thus poisoned, we go on blissfully to see to it that no "immorality" occurs on the screen. Any suggestion that the government should finance the production of movies and radio programs which would enlighten and improve the minds of our people would be met again with indignation and accusations in the name of freedom and idealism.'

Although these words were written fifty years ago, in his book *The Sane Society*, they seem uncannily applicable to the English-speaking world of 2007. A German intellectual who

moved to the USA in 1934, Fromm was a Marxist, a psychoanalyst and a Buddhist. He argued above all things for joy in
life rather than the living death that he perceived around him
in the affluent post-war USA. For him, the choice in Fifties
America was 'To Have or To Be'. Citing Marx's notion that
'a man is the one who *is* much, not the one who *has* much',
Fromm emphasised the extent to which material possessions
end up controlling us. He claimed that we have become
Marketing Characters, 'based on experiencing oneself as a
commodity, and one's value not as "use value" but
"exchange value" … his value depends on his success,
depends on his saleability, depends on approval by others'.

Since Fromm, the measurement of personality characteristics in order to select whom to employ has become a
billion-pound industry. Although he was writing before the
replacement of manufacturing by a service economy, Fromm
anticipated the dangers: 'Skill and equipment for performing
a given task are not sufficient; one must be able to "put one's
personality across" in competition with many others in
order to have success … a person is not concerned with his
or her life and happiness, but with becoming saleable … The
identity crisis of modern society is actually the crisis
produced by the fact that its members have become selfless
instruments, whose identity rests upon their participation in

the corporations.' Indeed, there is good evidence that, as physical strength has ceased to become important in occupations, social skills have become crucial. Studies show that just being bright does not predict success: it must be accompanied by characteristics such as Machiavellianism and chameleonism. This way of being is liable to corrupt personal relationships beyond the office (not to mention *The Office* of David Brent, the TV series by Ricky Gervais). 'What matters to the marketing character ... is perhaps the prestige or the comfort that things give, but things per se have no substance. They are utterly expendable, along with friends or lovers, who are expendable too, since no deeper tie exists to any of them.' Many years before the birth of Bridget Jones or her male equivalent, he put his finger on the damage this did to intimate relationships: 'A great deal of what goes under the name of love is a seeking for success, for approval. One needs someone to tell one not only at four o'clock in the afternoon but also at eight and at ten and at twelve: "You're fine, you're alright, you are doing well" ... One also proves one's value by choosing the right person; one needs to be the latest model oneself, but one then has a right also and a duty to fall in love with the latest model ... People do not see that the main question is not: "Am I loved?" Which is to a large extent the question: "Am I approved of? Am I protected? Am I admired?" The main question is: "Can I love?"'

This character is a recipe for emotional distress. It creates someone who, unconsciously according to Fromm, is 'a passive, empty, anxious, isolated person for whom life has no meaning and who is profoundly alienated and bored. If one asks these people ... whether they feel unhappy and bored they answer, "Not at all, we're completely happy. We go on trips, we drink, we eat, we buy more and more for ourselves. You aren't bored doing that!" ... in fact, the anxious, bored alienated person compensates for his anxiety [and depression] by a compulsive consumption.'

It is a dreadfully dull form of non-existence. 'Boredom comes from the fact that man has become purely an instrument, that he cultivates no initiative, that he feels not responsible, that he feels like a little cog in a machine that someone could replace with another at any time ... he tries to compensate for it – through consumption.' In accord with his colleagues in the Frankfurt School at the beginning of the last century, Fromm maintained that the tedium is worsened by the mechanisation of domestic and manufacturing life. 'He does indeed save time with his machines, but after he has saved time, then he does not know what to do with it. Then he is embarrassed and tries to kill this saved time in a

respectable way. To a large extent our entertainment industry, our parties and leisure activities are nothing but an
attempt to do away with the boredom of waiting in a
respectable manner ... necrophilia ... is the state of being
attracted to that which is dead.' People who live to Have
become emotionally necrophile.

The consumption and emotional pathology (anxiety
and depression) feed off each other: 'The more anxious
he becomes, the more he must consume, and the more he
consumes, the more anxious he becomes.' Consumption
causes the pathology partly because it holds up the false
promise that fixing an internal lack can be done by an external means, and partly because the process of working, by
which we earn the money to pay for the goods, is itself alien-
ating. We are liable to be rendered helpless and small by the
larger processes in the organisations for which we work
(whether freelance or as staff members); participation in
society is blocked by workaholia and by the carapaces
beneath which the Marketing Character hides. We become
addicted to status symbols, so that 'there is an enormous
fear in many social circles of not moving up, of losing the
position that one has attained. The fear that one's own wife
and friends will judge one as a "failure" if one does not
reach what the others reach.'

Although evolutionary psychology has sought to present addiction to this sliding scale of power, status and wealth as natural and inevitable, Fromm believes it is nothing of the kind. It just creates the bottomless pit of needs which keep economic growth going: 'By their nature, [socially generated] greed and the desire to have are characterized by their limitlessness. Physiological needs are limited by nature. We might be a little hungry or tremendously hungry, but at some point we are full.' Fromm the Marxist leaves no room for confusion in identifying where the blame for this grim scenario lies: 'What the economy needs most of all for its own operation is that people buy, buy and buy again, since there is otherwise no constantly growing demand for goods that industry can produce and must produce to an ever-growing degree if it wants to multiply its capital. For that reason, industry compels people by all means of temptation to consume more.'

Fromm follows this analysis through to its logical conclusion: that we live in a profoundly sick society. Whereas psychiatry measures emotional distress as deviation from the social norm, Fromm maintains that it should be analysed according to universal criteria. He proposes a definition of sanity which is applicable to individuals in all societies: relatedness, transcendence, rootedness, sense of identity, morality based on realistic rather than mythical ideas, and first-hand experiencing rather than the depersonalised, second-hand living that is so common in our society.

If someone is living in a society which derides these ways of Being in favour of Having, then deviation from that crazy norm is not mad – it's the society that needs fixing. Emotional well-being, writes Fromm, 'cannot be defined in terms of the adjustment of the individual to his society, but on the contrary … must be defined in terms of the adjustment of society to the needs of man'. A decade before the likes of R D Laing had declared the mad sane and the sane mad, Fromm was questioning the validity of conventional psychiatric wisdom: 'Nothing is more common than the idea that we, the people living in the Western world of the twentieth century, are eminently sane. Even the fact that a great number of individuals in our midst suffer from more or less severe forms of emotional distress produces little doubt with respect to the general standard of our emotional well-being. We are sure that by introducing better methods of mental hygiene we shall improve still further the state of our emotional well-being, and as far as individual mental disturbances are concerned, we look at them as strictly individual incidents, perhaps with some amazement that so many of these incidents should occur in a culture which is supposedly so sane. Can we be so sure that we are not deceiving ourselves? Many an inmate of an insane asylum is convinced that everybody else is crazy, except himself. Many a severe neurotic believes that his compulsive rituals or his hysterical outbursts are normal reactions to somewhat abnormal circumstances. What about ourselves?'

Fromm goes on to adduce, as evidence of our collective insanity, the fact that we killed about one hundred million people in wars during the twentieth century. He points to the increases in suicide, alcoholism and homicide that accompany urbanisation. He also casts doubt on the emotional well-being of our economics: 'We live in an economic system in which a particularly good crop is often an economic disaster, and we restrict some of our agricultural productivity in order to "stabilise the market", although there are millions of people who do not have the very things we restrict, and who need them badly. Right now our economic system is functioning very well, because, amongst other reasons, we spend billions of dollars per year to produce armaments. Economists look with some apprehension to the time when we stop producing armaments, and the idea that the state should produce houses and other useful and needed things instead of weapons, easily provokes accusations of endangering freedom and individual initiative.'

Even if you are not, I, at least, am astonished by how true of today are Fromm's claims about the USA in 1955. Just try making an analysis of Britain in 2007 which will seem as true in 2055. David Ingleby, in his introduction to the 1991 Routledge Classics edition of *The Sane Society*, aptly stresses how such analyses have fallen out of fashion: 'Grand generalisations about what is wrong with our culture and how to put it right are, nowadays, more often to be found on the shelves of alternative bookshops than in the university library. Intellectuals today are either pragmatically occupied with making a living, or immersed in a sort of refined hopelessness; like neurotics who have been disappointed by one failed therapy after another, they have resigned themselves to one counsellor who has always had time for them – their despair ... The loss of intellectual confidence in the direction of our civilisation has been accompanied by a loss of faith in the familiar stories within which we used to diagnose its problems and how they should be set right ... the depoliticisation of politics ... the party intellectuals have been put out to grass, and replaced by marketing consultants.'

Apart from this lamentable general shift away from social analysis, Ingleby also points to two aspects of Fromm's work which led to its being shunned by his peers. Few characteristics are more likely to lead to academic rejection than being widely read by the public, and Fromm's books achieved considerable popular success (rule number one: do not expect to be loved by your academic and clinical colleagues if you write a best-seller). But equally important, Fromm spanned several different domains in social science, including psychoanalysis, Marxist sociology and religious studies. Whilst embracing their fundamentals, he also criticised all of them and offered his own views instead. This meant that he had no single discipline rooting for him, and each of them feeling injured by his use of other disciplines as well as their own (rule number two: do not expect to be loved unless you politic within a discipline to cultivate a power base). Ingleby concludes that the forgetting of Fromm's remarkable oeuvre is part of the 'planned obsolescence of ideas' in modern life, so he has to be rediscovered all over again, including the idea of putting 'a whole culture on the couch' (my own work is a perfect illustration of this; although my book *Britain on the Couch* is jam-packed with Frommian thinking, I am ashamed to say that I had not read *The Sane Society* when I wrote it, and suffered from the sad illusion that my ideas were in some respects original).

Whilst commending Fromm's prophetic truths, Ingleby points out that the analysis is far from flawless (see endnote) but for all these, and doubtless many other criticisms (eg from the political Right), for me the really interesting thing about Fromm is that the most crucial elements of his analysis have been subsequently supported by scientific studies during the last fifteen years or so. In 1955 he bemoaned the fact that there was no good evidence available to test his theories: 'What is the incidence of mental illness in the various countries of the Western world? It is a most amazing fact that there are no data which answer this question. Whilst there are exact comparative statistical data on material resources, employment, birth and death rates, there is no adequate information about mental illness.' That is no longer true, and the WHO study of 2004 strongly supports his condemnation of the USA: with 26 per cent of its citizens suffering emotional distress in the previous twelve months, that nation is by far the most afflicted, just as Fromm predicted it would be. But perhaps even more exciting, a little-noticed body of studies has also directly tested Fromm's hypotheses and found confirmation of them in a wide variety of nations.

The evidence that materialism causes emotional distress

In 1993, the American psychologists Tim Kasser and Richard Ryan published a paper with the title 'A dark side of the American dream'. Using a specially developed 'Aspiration Index', they found that American students who put financial success ahead of motives like their emotional development, a happy family life and wanting to make the world a better place were significantly less emotionally well off. In particular, such students suffered more depression and anxiety, and they reported less of a sense of vitality and self-expression in their lives.

To check that this finding was not just a quirk of financially driven students, Kasser and Ryan studied a sample of eighteen-year-olds not at university and obtained similar results. Since the publication of that paper, along with a number of colleagues and following considerable refinement of the methods, they have studied thousands of people in a wide variety of countries and proved beyond reasonable doubt that materialistic motivation is to ill-being what smoking is to lung cancer. As we shall see, and just as Erich Fromm predicted, in all the fourteen countries studied so far and regardless of gender or age, materialism increases the risk of depression, anxiety, substance abuse, narcissism and the feeling that your life is joyless. However, just as not all smokers die prematurely of a smoking-related disease, so with materialism: it is possible to be both materialistic and to have emotional well-being.

In subsequent studies, Kasser (I shall use his name as a generic term for the authorship of studies he has done with colleagues) expanded the aspirations measured to include concerns with image (social and physical) and the desire for fame. Coupled with financial success, these aspirations constituted what he called 'extrinsic' motivations and goals, ones that rely on external rewards and praise from others. In a series of studies it was soon discovered that people who aspire to one of these (money, good image, fame) also tend to aspire to the others. This was true in Russian and German students as well as American ones. A community sample of New Yorkers ranging in age from eighteen to seventy-nine were assessed according to the revised Aspiration Index. Those with materialist aspirations were more likely to suffer depression, anxiety and lifelessness, as well as being at greater risk of common physical symptoms, such as headaches and sore throats.

These findings were repeated for an American student sample. In this case the students were asked to keep a diary, and the diaries revealed that materialists are also more prone to narcissism. Such people are liable to be vain, expect special treatment and crave admiration, and are often manipulative or hostile towards others. Consumerism encourages these traits ('Have it your way'; 'Want it? Get it!') and materialists were more likely to agree with statements such as 'I am more capable than other people' and 'I wish somebody would write my biography one day'. Given how unhappy materialists seemed to be, three different studies went on to investigate patterns of the use of 'drugs of solace' – cigarettes, alcohol, marijuana and hard drugs. Sure enough, materialistic young people were much more likely to use all of these frequently. One limitation of the Aspiration Index was that it presented subjects with a fixed set of alternatives, so Kasser now developed an instrument which allowed them to list their personal goals in their own words. A further series of studies involving more than 500 subjects reproduced the basic finding of the Aspiration Index: materialists of all ages and of both genders were significantly more miserable and liable to display physical symptoms.

Kasser's group were not the only ones investigating these matters. A study of more than 700 twelve- to twenty-year-olds found that those who aspired to material goals such as having expensive possessions, wearing expensive clothes and being pretty or handsome were significantly more at risk of most psychological problems. For example, they were one-and-a-half times more at risk of narcissism or of having disturbed personal relationships with friends or lovers.

Studies by market researchers also supported Kasser's findings: four different surveys found that materialists were
more prone to depression and anxiety. Other market
researchers, between them surveying thousands of people,
found that materialists report greater dissatisfaction with
their lives and less happiness.

Since all these studies were carried out in the USA, it was
possible that the results only applied to them. However, the
same materialism-misery correlation has been identified
using the Aspiration Index amongst samples of students in
Britain, Denmark, Germany, India, Russia, Singapore and
South Korea. Using similar methods, the correlation has
been found in samples of adults in Australia, China, Turkey
and Canada. Finally, a review of studies of more than 7,000
university students in forty-one countries showed that a
strong aspiration for financial success is accompanied by
reduced life satisfaction.

Since these findings are so robust and ubiquitous – there
is little doubt that materialism is strongly correlated with
depression, anxiety, substance abuse, narcissistic personality
traits and lifelessness – it is curious that they are rarely
referred to in reviews of the causes of emotional distress. If
a gene had been discovered correlating with these problems
it would have been given massive global publicity. I shall

return to this point, but for now I restrict myself to the following: just as it was strange that governments took so long to take effective action against tobacco companies once it was known beyond doubt that smoking is the major cause of cancer and one of the greatest preventable health hazards known to public medicine, so it seems peculiar that governments in the English-speaking world try to persuade voters to put the pursuit of material goals at the heart of our personal and national lives. This is all the stranger given that most of us believe that well-being should be a high governmental priority and that such policies would be vote-winners. A recent survey of Britons showed that fully 80 per cent of us would prefer our government to put well-being before wealth in formulating policy.

Returning to Kasser's research, the next question was why materialism correlates with emotional distress. In accord with a large body of evidence, his explanation begins with the claim that humans have four basic needs: to feel safe and secure; to feel competent; to feel connected to others; and to feel autonomously and authentically engaged in their work and play. The research shows that well-being increases when these needs are met and decreases when they are not.

Insecurity as a cause of materialism

Few subjects are more likely to make us feel insecure than thinking about our own death. To test whether materialism is triggered by insecurity, therefore, Kasser asked one sample of students to write short essays about listening to music and another to write about the feelings their own death aroused in them and what they thought might happen after it. Both groups then projected themselves fifteen years into the future and estimated how much money they would have, how much they would spend on pleasure purchases and the likely value of their major possessions. The sample in which fear of death had been evoked by their essay topic were significantly more materialistic in future expectations, hoping for larger incomes and more opulent possessions. In a second study, after two samples had written their essays on death or music, they were set a hypothetical task in which they had to choose between chopping down a forest for profit or maintaining it in an ecologically sustainable fashion. Again, exposure to death made that sample significantly more materialistic (tree-chopping).

Self-doubt, a form of insecurity, has also been shown to correlate with materialism. In one study, Americans who were beginners at tennis but also had a strong desire to succeed were more likely than more expert and self-confident players to wear expensive branded tennis clothes. This suggests that self-doubters may sometimes resort to high-status purchases to compensate for their feared incapacities. A more recent experiment established that self-doubters are more materialistic and that when these doubts were stimulated by the researchers, they became even more so. The same was found for 'anomie' (the sense that there are no social norms against which to define yourself, of being cut adrift without any compass). At the outset, anomic people were more likely than the non-anomic to fill their sense-of-value void with materialism. When their anomie was experimentally stimulated, they became still more materialistic.

To dig deeper in the materialist psyche, Kasser also did an in-depth study of students' dreams. Whereas nearly one-fifth of the materialists dreamt of death, it barely figured in the dreams of non-materialists. Likewise, falling – being out of control, with nothing to hold on to, suggesting insecurity – featured in 15 per cent of materialists' dreams, whereas it was present in only 3 per cent of the dreams of the non-materialists. Finally, there was an intriguing difference in the way the materialists and non-materialists dealt with frightening objects in their dreams. The non-materialists might turn a dangerous-seeming rhinoceros or giant purple poodle into an unfrightening character by attributing a benign motive to it; the materialists never did this, always seeing threatening figures as unalterably so.

If this study, together with the experiments showing the link between increased fear of death and increased material-ism, establishes that insecurity and materialism are common bedfellows, they do not explain why it is stronger in some of us than in others. One reason is childhood maltreatment. Materialists are more likely to have been starved of love (see below) and to have had divorced parents. One study meas-ured materialism in 261 twenty- to thirty-two-year-old adults. It was significantly more common in the 96 adults whose parents had divorced. Further analysis revealed that this materialism was due to the decline in love and nurtu-rance towards the children that the marital disharmony and fissure had caused, rather than to any increase in the financial hardship that often also resulted. Not that poverty is unimportant.

Several studies suggest that materialism is higher amongst children raised in poor homes, for obvious enough reasons: if you grow up not sure of where the next meal is coming from, it is liable to make you focus on material goals – survival materialism. On the global scale, actual wealth or the lack of it also helps to explain why levels of materialism vary between nations. In a study of 50,000 people from forty different nations of all sorts, people in poorer ones were generally more materialistic. Likewise, in a study of 9,000 adults from thirty-seven different cultures, women were more materialistic in their preferences when choosing a partner – they wanted a rich man – if they lived in a society where there was less opportunity to become educated and thus able to fend for themselves.

All of which suggests that insecurity triggers materialism, whether caused by family background, social class or national economics. Materialism is pursued both as a protection against insecurity and as a way of coping with it.

Materialists have poorer relationships

The materialistic are one-and-a-half times as likely to have personality disorders as the non-materialistic, and such people do not fare well in relationships. In a sample of 200 students, Kasser found that materialists' relationships were shorter-lasting and more negative. In another sample of 500 students, during the previous six months materialists were more likely to have argued with, insulted and sworn at their partner, in the process pushing, grabbing, shoving and physically hurting. This was even after pre-existing aggressive tendencies had been taken into account. In other studies, materialists have been found more likely to be alienated from others in their relationships. They agree with statements such as 'In order to relate to others, I often have to put on a mask' and 'I often feel detached from my social environment'. In Kasser's in-depth study of dream themes, the materialists more often reported active avoidance of intimacy and connectedness to others, and dreamt of conflict or rancour with lovers.

A major reason for this unhappy state of their affairs is that putting a high value on wealth, status and image leads the materialists to devalue intimate relationships and involvement in the community. They are less likely to endorse statements such as 'I will express my love for special people', 'I will have a committed, intimate relationship' and 'I will help others improve their lives'. One study, of forty different cultures, suggested that materialists tend *not* to subscribe to values which make for good relationships, such as loyalty, forgiveness and helpfulness. In making decisions about people, including in their social lives, they put the pursuit of status or money ahead of decency or other attributes likely to result in intimacy or friendship. This is illustrated by an experiment with four- to five-year-old boys. Half watched a programme with no advertisements and half watched the same one, but with two ads for a toy. They were all then shown pictures of two equally attractive-looking boys, one of whom was holding the advertised toy and described as 'not so nice', the other holding no toy but said to be 'a nice boy'. Twice as many children who had watched the ads said they wanted to play with the boy holding the toy, despite his not-niceness. This suggests that materialistic desires will override clear signals that another person will not be a pleasant playmate, even in small children.

By the end of childhood, the average American child will have seen 200,000 TV advertisements; materialists watch more television and therefore more ads, with a lust for status and wealth as a result, and this may lead them to make bad decisions when deciding whom to choose as a sexual partner or friend. Being close to or caring for others is not rewarded by status or money, so the materialistic downgrade it as an activity and do not appreciate care or intimacy offered them by others. If a materialist does desire truly loving relationships with friends, lovers or offspring, it sets up a big conflict with their desire to put material gain first. Most disastrous of all, it results in a manipulative misuse of others as pawns to be moved around the chessboard, as things rather than people.

Materialists have particular traits that make them especially prone to reification, being considerably less generous and more selfish, liable to ignore the human needs of others.

Asked in one study to spend a hypothetical windfall, they would use three times more of it on themselves than the non-materialists, giving only one-third as much to charities or friends. Another study found that they were less prepared to help others out, whether by lending money or doing voluntary work. They are also less interested in others' viewpoints, being more ready to criticise others without understanding what it is like to be in their place, or to insist on their own view if they believe that they are in the right without hearing the other side of the argument.

Kasser showed the extent to which they view others as pawns. Materialistic students in India, the USA and Denmark agreed with statements such as 'I like to be with cool people because it helps me to look cool too' and 'If a friend can't help me to get ahead in life, I usually end the friendship'. In an experiment providing opportunities to cooperate or exploit, materialists were liable to be the exploiters. Materialists are statistically significantly more likely to be Machiavels ('machs'), a trait measured by a questionnaire which has shown many times over that such people are cynical, distrustful, self-centred and manipulative. They believe that you should avoid telling people why you did something unless it is to your advantage, that others are lazy and deceptive (anyone who completely trusts them is seen as asking for trouble) and that lying is acceptable. When a sample of 250 students were assessed, those who were machs were also more likely to be materialists. What is more, materialists are also more likely to be hyper-competitive, desperate to be first in everything they do, with winning as an end in itself and prepared if necessary to cause extreme harm to others or themselves if that is necessary to achieve it – a dehumanisation. They are also more liable to be chameleons ('high self-monitors'), again manipulating themselves or others like objects, and to suffer Personality Disorder.

Of course, not all the materialists are also Machiavellian, personality-disordered, hyper-competitive chameleons but the higher likelihood of them being so makes it probable that if the issue were tested, their marriages would be more likely to end in divorce. Their relationships with friends are manipulative and superficial, and with their children, controlling and insensitive – bad news for all concerned. Blaming the collapse of the family and the decline of communities on the decline of religion and emergence of louche morals is a favourite habit of the political Right. Materialistic values, driven by Selfish Capitalism, look far more significant.

Materialists are more inauthentic and lacking in autonomy

The thousands of people who have filled out Kasser's Aspiration Index who emerge as materialistic tend to place a low value on self-expression and autonomy. They disagree with statements such as 'I will choose what I do, instead of being pushed along by life' and 'I will follow my interests and curiosity where it takes me'. Studies by other researchers have found the same: that if money, fame or appearances are important to someone, they will be unlikely to say that understanding themselves or being true to themselves 'no matter what' are important to them. Kasser found that materialists (in India and the USA) agreed with statements such as 'I'm less concerned with what work I do than what I get for it' and 'I am strongly motivated by the grades I can earn' (in exams). They disagreed with 'The more difficult the problem, the more I enjoy trying to solve it' and 'I want my work to provide me with opportunities for increasing my knowledge and skills'. Asked to list their two commonest work and leisure activities, and the two friends they spend most time with, materialists more frequently listed boredom, feeling trapped and feeling unengaged in connection with them. Another study, of American and South Korean students, asked about the most satisfying event they had experienced in recent times. If money, popularity or luxury had been important during the event, the students were less positive and more negative about the experience.

These findings go to the heart of materialist psychology: it is driven by a desire for extrinsic rewards and praise nurtured in materialists by parents and wider social forces. These are eventually 'introjected', taken to be part of oneself, creating guilt or anxiety if disobeyed, and experienced as an instruction to conform – compulsively so. The opposite of this is known as intrinsic values, where interest, enjoyment and being challenged are paramount, activities done for their own sake, for their 'flow'. Extrinsic goals and motives increase vulnerability to boredom, depression, anxiety and personality disorder.

Low self-esteem, materialism and watching television

Materialists are more likely than non-materialists to have low self-esteem. If self-esteem depends on achieving materialistic goals, it becomes vulnerable to wild fluctuations. Studies show that even if goals are achieved, the boost to self-esteem is short-lived and, in face of failure, more liable to go down. If the worth you place upon your self is contingent upon how well you do in an exam or the size of your annual bonus, it will fall if you do not achieve what you hoped for. Since no one always gets the results they want and since (as we shall see) materialists are anyway likely to have bloated ambitions, it's not surprising that they have low self-esteem – nor that they are prone to narcissistic or other defences against feeling it. Materialists who suffer a reverse may deal with the drop in their worth by simply saying to themselves, 'I am a wonderful person, I deserve to be the object of everyone's admiration' – despite all the evidence to the contrary. Narcissism apart, people with such unstable, shaky self-esteem use other ways to distract themselves and others from uncomfortable evidence that contradicts their bloated estimate of their accomplishments. They will have an exaggerated liking for people who praise them and an equally excessive hostility towards critics.

People with stable high self-esteem, based on authentic self-appraisal rather than rewards, are less likely to employ these defensive manoeuvres and self-deceptions than those with unstable high self-esteem. Indeed, several experiments show that when people are praised for aspects of their authentic selves rather than their achievements, they are less defensive. If praised by someone who is perceived as accepting of who they are, people are also less defensive than if praised by someone perceived as judging by achievements.

Materialists' low self-esteem derives from exaggerated ideas of what wealth and possessions can deliver. Materialistic students asked to characterise wealthy people suppose them to be clever, cultured and successful in everything. Many materialists feel that they do not live up to that standard, and are liable to find a discrepancy between what they hope for and what they are actually like. A major source of the unrealistic ideals is television. Studies of viewers in Australia, Denmark, Finland, Hong Kong, India and the USA show that materialists watch more TV. Since programmes are saturated with exceptionally attractive people living abnormally opulent lives, expectations of what is 'normal' are raised. And in between the programmes come the advertisements. As the creators of these visual confections freely admit, one of their main objectives is to create a sense of dissatisfaction with existing possessions so that viewers are persuaded to buy new, 'better' ones; ergo, heavy viewers are particularly at risk of a constant sense that they are inadequate, especially if they judge themselves by what they own (which, in turn, they are more likely to do if they are the sort of person who watches a lot of TV).

Evidence of the role television plays in nurturing materialism comes from a substantial tranche of studies. Firstly, heavy TV watchers are more likely than light watchers to be dissatisfied with their lives. This was so in a study of elderly Americans, and the heavies also had low morale and felt they were worse off than other people. Another study, of 1,200 adults in the USA, Canada, Australia, China and Turkey, illuminated the processes involved. Having established that materialists are less satisfied by their standards of living and with their lives, it also found that they watched more TV, and when asked to compare their lives to characters in programmes, they were more negative about the contrast. In the American sample, materialists' relentless exposure to images of wealth and beauty was particularly likely to spill over and poison the rest of their lives, beyond the sitting room. Other studies show that people often switch on the TV as a way of changing their mood, and viewers describe it as one of the most relaxing of all their leisure activities (in the short term; just as eating some chocolate is a delicious way to – very briefly – cheer oneself up, with longer-term consequences ignored or unconsidered). Whilst this works fine for people who are selective in how and when they watch, it is less so for people who use TV to avoid being conscious of their distress.

A review of seventy-nine studies shows that people who feel bad about themselves seek out ways to avoid self-awareness, not just through TV or other fictions, of course, but also through drugs, alcohol and work. Sundry other studies also show that heavy TV-watchers are more prone to feel lonely and to be socially isolated, a vicious circle. We watch because we want company, we lack company because we watch too much rather than getting out and meeting people. Too much TV-watching and too little socialising both lower self-esteem and increase depression, making us less likely to socialise, more likely to switch on the box, making us still lonelier.

A particular reason for escapist watching is to avoid feeling a failure, and ironically this sometimes does work in the short term (in the longer term it serves only to highlight the viewer's inadequacy compared with the glamorous folk they watch). In one experiment, students who had been shown the results of a test which they had been bogusly shown to fail (the results were fixed) were more likely to watch TV and to feel better for doing so than those who had been told that they had succeeded. Another experiment found the same for subjects who had been played depressing rather than uplifting music – watching TV was commoner after being depressed by the music and did elevate mood. The explanation seems to be that, in the case of people who felt bad because they thought they had failed, they used TV to escape from themselves, selves that they felt had fallen short of a desired (ironically, partly television-fostered in the first place) standard.

A crucial element in the impact of TV is advertisements. Much evidence has emerged to suggest this since Vance Packard's largely anecdotal book *The Hidden Persuaders* was published in 1957. In the first place, the version of reality portrayed on TV does not equate with the real world. A study of American TV content, for example, established that about three-quarters of TV characters are male, most are single, white, middle- to upper-class and in their twenties and thirties. The women characters tend to represent romantic or family interests. Oddly, whilst only one-third of male leading characters in TV dramas intend to, or have, married, this is true of two-thirds of their female counterparts. About 40 per cent of characters in American dramas are employed in professional and managerial roles (compared with 20 per cent in American reality). A remarkable 20 per cent of characters are employed in law enforcement (compared with less than 1 per cent in reality). Not surprisingly, given these distortions, heavy TV viewers are significantly more likely than light viewers to overestimate when asked to guess these real-world percentages.

The cumulative effects of all this have been demonstrated on our attitudes to sex, violence and larceny. In a seminal 1970s study, American psychologist Douglas Kenrick barged in on male students whilst they were watching the 'babe'-packed TV programme *Charlie's Angels* and asked them to rate a picture of an averagely attractive female student. For comparison, he did the same with students watching babe-free shows. He found that the babe-watchers gave the average student a lower score, suggesting that, at least for male students, standards are raised by exposure to babe-packed programming, a conclusion borne out by further experiments. Slides were shown to three groups of male students, respectively of *Playboy* centrefolds, averagely attractive women and abstract art. Sure enough, the *Playboy* group rated an average-looking woman lower than the other groups did. For his next trick, Kenrick repeated the study but this time the men were asked afterwards to rate their partners in terms of attractiveness and how much they loved them. The effect transferred to real relationships: the *Playboy*-affected men rated their partners lower. Further evidence of this from real life is that male American secondary school and university teachers have higher divorce rates than primary school teachers. The higher rate was ascribed to the contrast the men were experiencing between the nubility of their pupils and the relative undesirability of their wives, causing dissatisfaction. In the same way, if you are male and afflicted by materialism you are that much more likely to watch large amounts of TV containing sexy women, setting up a contrast that is unfavourable to your partner.

Turning to the effect on women's mood, Kenrick found that when women were shown slides of models or of average-lookers, models lowered their mood. This added to a growing body of evidence that women exposed to images of very attractive other women suffer decreased self-esteem. Indeed, so powerful is the effect of being unusually attractive that such women are more likely to suffer social rejection from female peers, who are made to feel bad just by their presence. Discontent of women with their bodies in English-speaking nations is considerable, and TV watching has been shown to be closely linked to both eating disorders and obesity. A meta-analysis of twenty-five studies demonstrated its impact on girls vulnerable to eating disorders. And the effect is by no means confined to the English-speaking world: a study in Fiji demonstrated a dose-dependent relationship between amount of TV viewed and eating disorders – the more TV, the more disordered – and a Chinese study found that increased viewing correlated with obesity.

Greater affluence ends starvation, yet with it comes TV, which fosters both self-starvation and obesity.

An adjacent body of evidence shows the causes and effects of magazine images of women. In a series of studies of fluctuations in the Thin Standard (desirable bust-and-hip/waist ratio) during the twentieth century, the American psychologist Brett Silverstein began by showing that, based on photographs of women in popular magazines, in the mid-1920s and from the mid-1960s to the present day, standards became very thin. A bustier shape was in vogue in 1900–20 and 1930–1960. In explaining these fluctuations, Silverstein pointed to the fact that in most societies men are more likely to be the high achievers. At the same time, curvaceous women are perceived to be less competent and less intelligent than non-curvaceous ones and, therefore, women who want to be successful might minimise their visible femininity. Could female aspirations to male achievements be linked to varying popularity in the Thin Standard?

First of all, Silverstein established that thinness and achievement are connected in women's minds. Modern women who preferred smaller breasts and smaller buttocks, as demonstrated by their responses to silhouettes of female figures, were also more likely to choose 'masculine' careers and desire high academic achievement. For a historical dimension, Silverstein also showed that past medical case reports related to eating disorders uncovered strivings for intellectual or academic achievement in every single girl or woman studied. For much of the twentieth century it was extremely difficult for women to achieve any recognition at all, and the desire to seem more physically masculine may have been intensified. Disordered eating in modern girls is particularly common amongst academic high achievers. Girls from fee-paying schools are more at risk than those at state schools, and upper-class girls are more likely than lower-class girls to desire to be slimmer (whatever their actual weight). This is related to parental expectations, which are themselves influenced by wider society. Silverstein demonstrated that women undergraduates were more likely to engage in binge eating if they felt that their mothers were dissatisfied with their career performance. Amongst women who had brothers, bingeing was more likely if the father reported that his son was more intelligent than his daughter. A further study of women students proved that those who had male sex role aspirations were more at risk of eating disorders. Likewise, women who said that they wished they had been born a boy were more at risk. In short, women who aspire to traditionally male-only achievements are more likely to aspire to a male body shape. Silverstein's coup de grace was to correlate the bust-to-waist ratios of models in magazine photographs since the beginning of the century with the proportion of women working as professionals at the beginning of each decade up to 1980. When women were pushing harder to be taken seriously, academically and professionally, a thinner body shape closer to the male one was in vogue.

Whilst Silverstein's work demonstrates the importance of fluctuating gender roles and parental nurture, it may also suggest that magazine images influence women's assumptions about what is normal. Since materialist women are more likely to graze the pages of magazines in search of identities and possessions, they would be more influenced. This was shown in three more recent American studies. Most of the subjects in samples of female students said that they frequently looked at magazines as a way of envisioning what they might ideally look like, and some admitted that this led to unpleasant feelings of inadequacy by comparison with the gorgeous models. Half of 200 female students were shown advertisements for perfume and sportswear featuring stunning models, and the other half were shown adverts for similar products but containing no models. Although, overall, the model-exposed group did not rate themselves as less attractive than the other group as a result of exposure to the advertising, they did feel less satisfied with their looks: ads with models raised standards of what was attractive. Since materialists are more interested in this kind of media material, their consumption of it would make them more likely to be unhappy with their looks.

Taken together, the body of evidence described above shows how profoundly TV and magazines affect the self-esteem of women with regard to their appearance. But the proven effect of TV does not end there. Regarding violence, it used to be thought that only people whose childhoods had made them prone to it were made more likely to enact it by TV images. However, recent research has revealed that TV has an independent effect. When a large sample of Americans was followed over a seventeen-year period, the amount of time watching TV during adolescence and early adulthood by itself predicted who subsequently became violent. This was so even after taking into account other key predictors, such as how aggressive the subjects had been when young, parental maltreatment and coming from a low-income family. As a cause of the massive rise in violence throughout the developed world (Switzerland and Japan are the only exceptions), TV is clearly a major one. Increases in shoplifting and theft have also been proved to be caused by watching TV.

Hennigan took advantage of the fact that television in the USA was not introduced at the same time across the nation, but over a period of five years, to examine how its gradual introduction correlated with crime. She correlated FBI statistics for crime rates with the introduction of TV in sixty-eight cities where the sale of sets was extremely rapid once transmissions began (reaching half of all households during the first year). She compared rates of crime in thirty-four cities that had TV introduced in 1951 with thirty-four cities that were then TV-free. She found that rates of violence, burglary and car theft were unaffected a year later but rates of larceny rose significantly in the cities where TV was introduced. Hennigan made a further comparison in 1955. Again, the thirty-four cities that had previously had no TV but now had it saw an increase in the rate of larceny by the end of the first year after its introduction, compared with rates in the cities that had already had TV for four years, whose rate of increase did not markedly change. Hennigan estimated the degree of impact as follows: 'The impact of television on larceny seems to have been to increase it by at least 5 per cent in the year television saturation reached 50 per cent [of households].' She offered this interpretation of her findings: 'The lower classes and modest lifestyles were rarely portrayed on TV, yet the heaviest viewers have been and are poorer, less educated people. It is possible that in the 1950s television caused younger and poorer persons (the major perpetrators of theft) to compare their lifestyles and possessions with (a) those of wealthy television characters and (b) those portrayed in advertisements. Many of these viewers may have felt resentment and frustration over lacking the goods they could not afford, and some may have turned to crime as a way of obtaining the coveted goods and reducing any "relative deprivation".'

The finding that violence was unaffected by the introduction of TV could be explained by the fact that TV in those days was tamer and provided clear ethical guidelines (older British viewers will recall the moral homilies with which the cop show *Dixon of Dock Green* began and ended). It was some time before shows portrayed the graphic violent scenes we take for granted today. Hennigan argued that the increase in larceny back in the 1950s was unlikely to have been ascribable to direct imitation (known as 'social learning') of TV characters since portrayals of larcenists were rare. Rather it was the result of adverse upward social comparison, stimulating aspirations and entitlements to consumer goods and wealth that many viewers could not legally obtain.

Education and parenting as causes of materialism

In Michael Young's dystopia *The Rise of the Meritocracy*, published in 1958 and set in 2034, one's IQ test score and exam performance, not wealth or class, determine one's position in society. In Young's words, 'Intelligence has been redistributed between the classes and the nature of the classes changed. The talented have been given the opportunity to rise.' So sophisticated have the tests become that they can predict a subject's scores for the rest of their life at the age of three, even if they turn out to be a late developer. Those in the top 5 per cent are given special treatment, with schooling streamed from the beginning.

In the past, 'government by the people, of the people for the people meant government by old people, of young people, for old people'. The gerontocratic rule of the elderly has been abolished, so that hardly any of society's most powerful figures are over fifty, IQ usually diminishing in later life, it is found. In the new system, those who held high-ranking jobs but whose IQ has dropped in middle age are forced to accept posts as lowly mechanics, sometimes in the same company. Everyone is given a sort of five-yearly IQ MOT to ensure that they are at the right level in the employment hierarchy, because job allocation is strictly related to IQ scores: 'matching of intelligence and job in the various streams of society was everywhere demonstrated as the high-est expression of both efficiency and humanity'.

Inherited affluence has been abolished by huge taxes on capital wealth. Private schools have withered because they are no longer the Royal Road to university – state schools are far better because teachers there are paid far more. Where previously the children of the rich could be slid into the lower reaches of the professions through contacts, this is no longer possible. The brassy self-confidence of stupid chil-dren of clever or rich parents is exposed as unmerited by repeated testing, and they are forced to accept their true place at the bottom of society. This actually makes them happier because they were always liable to feel fraudulent by occupying jobs which were beyond their ability. Relative deprivation is also reduced by everyone ostensibly having equal pay, although in reality the elite are 130 times richer than the poorest through tax-free benefits such as housing, holidays and servants. 'What a change there has been!' writes Young. 'The distribution of rewards has become far more unequal and yet with less strife than before.' This sense of satisfaction is cunningly reinforced by increasing every-one's pay annually in line with the cost of living, on the prin-ciple that people always feel that 'enough' income is 10 per cent more than they currently earn.

Domestic service has been reintroduced as a widespread career for the low-IQ members of society, who act as nannies, cooks and cleaners to the high-IQ members. (In modern Britain most domestics are immigrants, but Young's prediction of a return to widespread use of servants by the middle classes was essentially correct.) 'There was no need for the drudgery to fall to the lot of the intelligent, it was much better left to the person who would not regard it as drudgery at all because she was not capable of anything higher ... domestic service could be restored once it was again accepted that some men were superior to others; and done without resentment because the inferior knew their betters had a great part to play in the world and beyond, and were glad to identify with them and wait on them.'

The driver of this meritocratic system is economic performance, and its greatest impediment is parental nepotism. 'For hundreds of years society has been a battleground between two great principles – the principle of selection by family and the principle of selection by merit.' In winning this battle in Young's dystopia, 'the need to subordinate everything else to the claims of production was so pressing that education was at last decisively reformed and the family torn away from the feudal embrace'. In the new system, whilst parents are always inclined to try to gain preferential treatment for their children, if they are told that theirs has a low IQ they console themselves with the thought that they may yet have other children of a higher IQ or that their grandchildren may be luckier: 'The greater the frustrations parents experience in their own lives, the greater their aspirations for their children.' The system has been tremendously successful in stimulating ambition in most of its members, especially the working classes. 'Every advance towards greater equality of opportunity in education ... stimulated aspiration ... [E]ach new opportunity did something to stimulate appetite.' Where once a poor man, such as a docker, had assumed that his son could only follow in a similar unskilled occupation, 'improvement of communications helped to root out such wickedness by advertising the standards of the wealthy and the glittering lives of thousands of people far beyond his own community to every child in the country. All subjective judgements about the status of different jobs were assimilated to the one national model'. (This seems like an especially prescient prediction of the role of TV in stimulating a one-size-fits-all, globalised consumer society, written as it was in the late 1950s before TV was as widespread and as international in its referents as today.)

Working-class disenchantment with this system was largely non-existent and when the few rebellious high-IQ people who sought to stir it up went about their rebellious business, they found that 'for the spark there was no timber'. The working classes were 'sharing in the stability of employment, intent on the interests of their children ... more and more parents began to harbour ambitions for their children rather than their class'. This is extraordinarily illuminatory of today. Forty years before New Labour's triumph, Young wrote that Labour politicians 'scrapped the appeal to working-class solidarity and concentrated on the middle class, partly to capture new sections of the electorate, more to keep pace with their own supporters, who had in their outlook moved upwards from their point of origin'.

Of course, the whole point of Young's book was to warn of the risks that meritocracy posed to our well-being. Educated at a child-centred, ultra-progressive school, Dartington Hall (oddly enough, my mother and Lucian Freud were his contemporaries there), Young was very unusual for a socialist of that era in recognising the pitfalls of the appropriation of education by national economic performance. Then, as now, few doubted that educating the masses was the key to social mobility. But as Young explained, 'stupid children' as well the intelligent would have their hopes raised by the prospect of education, only to have their self-regard shattered when the education system tested them and labelled them 'inferior'. This goes right to the heart of the problem of our new obsession with assessment and its central place in self-esteem. Countless studies show that people in English-speaking nations blow a rose-tinted bubble of positive illusions to keep uncomfortable reality at bay. We imagine that our friends like us more than they do, that bad things are less likely to happen to us than statistically likely. A ruthless and unquestionable assessment system pricks that bubble irreparably.

Evidence has accumulated that all too many of Young's dystopic speculations have come to pass. Compared with 1950, we spend much more of our childhood in classrooms, and for most children the competition is much fiercer. With the realisation by governments that education was crucial to economic growth, the average number of years' schooling in the developed nations doubled between 1913 and 1983. In most developed nations, the substantial increase in secondary and higher education occurred after 1950. Between 1950 and 1980 it almost doubled in France and Japan, whilst in other nations the main acceleration was in the 1980s. In the Netherlands, for example, the proportion of twenty-one-year-olds in higher education rose from 14 per cent to 32 per cent between 1975 and 1986. On average, half of nineteen-year-olds in developed nations are in some form of higher education today, and a quarter of twenty-one-year-olds, compared with a tiny fraction of these age groups before the Second World War. In Britain in 1979, one in eight school-leavers went on to higher education; today it is 40 per cent.

Although there is no doubt that standards of literacy and numeracy are higher than a century ago, there is evidence that in the last twenty years in Britain they have actually fallen, at least in children educated at state schools which have high numbers of children from low-income families. There is also good evidence that grade inflation has reduced the standards of secondary and graduate qualifications. However, at the top end of the scale competition has never felt tougher. In many cases it starts at birth. Parents reading modern baby manuals are encouraged to evaluate the 'progress' of their infants towards 'developmental mile-stones'. The competition to get baby weaned, potty-trained, walking and talking is extreme in some social circles. Penelope Leach, a child psychologist and best-selling author of baby manuals, has provided a telling critique of such hothousing. 'Child development is a process, not a race … major landmarks like walking and talking are important and exciting … The modern infant *is* human and therefore *will* become a biped and communicate in speech. She is not a better example of her species because she does these things at an earlier age than average ... We behave as if the child who walks earliest will walk fastest, as if exceptionally early single words predict meaningful later sentences, and as if children's prospects as intelligent, independent and socialised people can be improved by speeding them through the age-appropriate illiteracy, dependence or incontinence. It is not so and there is abundant evidence to prove it'.

The increased overall competitiveness in the higher echelons of the education system is only to be expected since for five decades enormous efforts have been made to encourage the participation of groups previously largely excluded from higher education – women, and children from low-income families. In Britain in the 1970s, one-quarter of graduates were female; today the proportion is half. It should also be recalled that it is only recently that access to universities became significantly dependent on academic prowess. Previously, the principal requirements were a public school education, being male and having parents wealthy enough to support you. With the post-war increase in competitiveness, grades at O level (and later, GCSE) and A level rose steadily, particularly sharply in the 1980s. Whilst it seems highly probable that this was due partly to a lowering of standards, it must also have been the result of more exam-focused schooling. This is well illustrated by the way grades have changed at Eton College (the 'top people's' school, as it is often dubbed in the newspapers). In the 1970s about half the boys were sons of alumni whereas today it is more merito-cratic – about 30 per cent. Boys who would once have been accepted, even though they would never be academically very able and dragged down the overall ranking of the school, are now weeded out by the rigorous entrance exam. The consequences of these new entry criteria, combined with tougher teaching, show in the results. In 1977, 31 per cent of Etonians obtained a grade D or worse in one of their A levels, whereas today hardly any do. In 1977, 46 per cent of boys achieved one B grade or better at A level. By 1995 the proportion was 84 per cent and today the average Etonian gets better than three A grades. This trend towards higher grades (one found in the system as a whole) has continued to the present day, with Eton always near the top of the league tables.

One stimulus for these changes was that competition for the top universities to which Old Etonians have traditionally gone had also increased, and students starting at those universities found the competitiveness substantially greater. Whereas many students in the 1970s spent little time doing academic work, industriousness increased steadily from the

1980s onwards. By the mid-1990s, students were twice as likely to graduate with a 2:1 or a first compared with the early 1970s. Whilst some of this increase was due to grade inflation, it is unlikely that the whole of the difference can be so explained. But such a rise is exactly what would be expected from increased competition, given the huge increases in the number of able women and children from low-income families.

Overall, then, two major changes have occurred in the educational life of young people since 1950: they spend a great deal more time at school, and their schooling is considerably more competitive, and from ever younger ages. Because these changes are so widely assumed to be 'a good thing' by all political parties and by the media, their potentially dire effect on the self-esteem and well-being of many children, both high and low achievers, is rarely discussed.

According to Diane Ruble, the most active researcher of this subject, social comparison starts young in life. 'Anyone who observes three-, four- and five-year-olds will see them make comparisons all the time. Sibling rivalry starts very young.' She has presented evidence that 'preschool children seem to want to make sure they are getting their fair share of rewards, readily engage in competition, and make overt comparison statements'. However, until about the age of seven, children are very indiscriminate in whom they choose to compare themselves with, as happy to pick an adult as they are a peer. They seem to have only a minimal grasp of the comparative dimensions for many characteristics and therefore are unaware that they may have done worse than others. Ruble concludes that 'Children's assessments of their relative performance in classroom are quite unrealistic until after their early school years'. There is usually a large discrepancy between their own view of their status, in terms of such skills as alphabet acquisition and reading, and their teacher's view. They ignore information about the performance of contemporaries and so feel no sense of inadequacy. They are much more likely to assess themselves by reference to their previous performances on a task – to judge that they have read a story better than last time they read it for themselves, not better than a peer has read it. They also compare more to absolute rather than relative standards – of sums they will say, 'I got them all right.' At this stage they are not backward in coming forward about their achievements. Comparing the utterances of three- to six-year-olds with seven- to nine-year-olds, Ruble found the younger ones more likely to give voice to their successes.

At the age of seven there comes a big change. In their utterances at this age, children are much less positive about their own performance. Indeed, successful children who parade their successes in front of their peers discover that they lose friends. As Ruble puts it, 'there is a shift from rather boorish braggadocio to questions requiring little self-disclosure'. But at the same time there is a steady increase in social comparing with peers as the means of self-evaluation, rather than using past personal performance or inappropriate others, like adults. If now more circumspect about their own, they are more likely to request information about peers' performances. As a result they become more realistic, and the gap between their appraisal of themselves and their teachers' appraisal closes. They become increasingly preoccupied with competition and beating peers, and teaching methods become increasingly designed to exploit this, using techniques that encourage public victories and defeats.

But these changes are not without their cost to the child's well-being. Perhaps because they do not compare with peers and are largely ignorant of their performance relative to them, according to Ruble 'preschool and primary grade children show impressive resilience in the face of failure. They maintain persistence, self-confidence and expectations of future success. By mid-elementary school [aged seven] however, such optimism and positive responses to failure largely disappear ... with increasing disinterest in school-related activities appearing as children progress through elementary school. When self-consciousness is induced [about their standard relative to other children], seven- to nine-year-old children are not satisfied unless their performance surpasses other children'. Ruble argues that 'because there are only a limited number of "winners" in any competitive system, children may experience a dissatisfaction with themselves ... Comparison can promote a sense of relative deprivation and inadequacy, affecting interpersonal relationships and self-esteem'. From age seven to nine, self-esteem, self-confidence and optimism decrease at school.

Ruble emphasises the crucial fact that schoolchildren who feel that they are failing (even though they may be doing well) seem not to be able to escape from the comparative system. She suggests ways in which they could try to escape, such as 'disengagement' – becoming less engaged with school activities. Another method is the development of anti-academic school cliques to provide a counter-culture with an alternative means of gaining self-esteem than the prevailing academic standards. But despite these evasions, the commonest effect of all is lowered self-esteem and the reason seems to be increased social comparison.

Ruble says that 'The drop in self-confidence and achievement expectancies found during the early school years may be due to the incorporation of comparative standards into the self-concept'. Children who do badly do more social comparing than those who are succeeding, because they are searching for clues as to where they are going wrong and because they feel uncertain. She goes on: 'children may develop a poor opinion of themselves because they compare frequently, or they may socially compare more because they have a poor opinion of themselves … They may begin to look for additional information but along the way the perception of the self as poor comes, in part, from negative conclusions they draw from social comparison information. Taken all together, the data suggest that the period from seven to nine years is a very important one for self-definition and self evaluation.' Children who do badly, as well as compounding the problem by increased social comparison, are more likely to show signs of learned helplessness – to act as if their actions cannot make any difference. Experimental studies bear this out. When children were given low scores (regardless of performance) on tests, they began to display signs of helplessness.

Crucial in all this is the unavoidability and objectivity of the comparisons in the classroom. By contrast, adults are often able 'to move the goalposts' if they are failing. Ruble illustrates this neatly with a study of 153 male and 84 female long-distance adult runners. They were classified into three groups: improving, declining and stable. Ruble discovered that the ones who were improving were eager to measure themselves by reference to the time they were taking over the course. By contrast, the runners whose performances were not changing or were declining avoided thinking about how fast they were going relative to past performances and to the whole field, and instead concentrated on how well they were doing compared with other runners of about the same standard. In this way they could avoid the uncomfortable fact that they were not improving and continue to feel good about themselves. But such redefinitions are not available to schoolchildren who are regularly assessed and told where they stand in their class or what grade they have achieved in exams, almost whatever steps they may take to avoid the process.

The problem starts even before the child has reached school, with patterns of parenting, encouraged by powerful social pressures. Richard Ryan distinguishes two ways in which parents socialise children. In the first, a controlling pattern is applied, pressurising the child to think, feel and behave using rewards, threats, deadlines and hectoring words. Love is conditional upon achievement of goals laid down by the parent – there is no love for the child that does not achieve them. By contrast, the supportive pattern of care takes the child's perspective, minimising pressure and encouraging it to find out for itself what it wants. Self-determination by the child is valued by the parent. In the child, these two patterns result in very different types of internal relationship with parental wishes, investigated in studies by Richard Ryan (often with his colleague Edward Deci, as well as Tim Kasser). Whereas 'introjection' entails the unquestioning acceptance of them, amounting to a compulsive need to obey parental injunctions, in 'identification' the child has actively decided in an act of volition to adopt a parental wish. In both cases parental values influence those of their children, but it happens in different ways.

With regard to a strong desire for financial success, a study of 140 eighteen-year-olds and their mothers found that if the latter had it, so did the former. But this was not a simple matter of learnt ideas. The key factor was whether the mother was cold and controlling, with love conditional on success; only then was the child more likely to ape the parent. Cold, conditional, controlling parenting has been shown many times over to induce parroted values. Tim Kasser followed up seventy-nine adults when aged thirty-one who had been studied at the age of five. Adults who had cold, controlling mothers were more likely to be achievement-chasers. That this is often specifically due to introjection rather than identification was tested in a pair of studies by Ryan.

In the first study, 110 American students of both sexes were asked whether parental love had been conditional on success in a particular field, such as sporting prowess. Students for whom love had been conditional were more likely to have experienced only short-lived pleasure when they succeeded, to feel shame and guilt following failures, to have lower self-esteem and to feel greater resentment towards parents. They were also more likely to have introjected parental dictates (measured as an internal compulsion to perform rather than a sense of choice with regard to that behaviour), and what is more, they were also likely to have enacted the specifically desired behaviour – to be fanatical sportsmen if so instructed, or to be people-pleasers if that was what was required. Finer data analysis showed that the conditionality of the parental love in itself did not lead to robotic enactment of the behaviour: there had to be introjection of it as well; pursuing parental goals did not happen in the offspring with conditionally loving parents who did not also feel an internal compulsion (introjection). Further analysis also revealed that the resentment towards parents was not caused by conditional love alone; the offspring needed to feel that there had been a lot of disapproval from parents with regard to the child's performance in the particular pursuit (eg sport or people-pleasing).

Ryan's second study provided strong evidence that this pattern passes down the generations. One hundred and twenty-four American mothers were asked how controlling or supportive both they and their own parents had been. The mothers who said that their parents had been controlling were more likely to have low self-esteem and ineffective ways of dealing with stress, such as dwelling on misfortunes. They were also more likely to describe their own parenting style as controlling, even though it was the way they had been cared for that had given them these problems. All these mothers had a student daughter, who was also interviewed. If the grandparent had been controlling, the student granddaughter was more likely to say that her mother had been controlling, providing additional evidence that the controlling style had passed down from grandparent to mother. In addition, the students were more likely to have low self-esteem and poor coping skills if their mother had been controlling.

These findings are strongly concordant with bodies of evidence regarding 'self-critical' depression and perfectionism. These have become especially common in girls. They may set themselves impossible standards, strive for excessive achievement and perfection, are often highly competitive and hard-working, making huge demands on themselves, yet never feel lasting satisfaction even if they succeed.

A child's drive to achieve can be overstimulated, which is also liable to trigger depression, if its parents compare it with inappropriate social models. For example, in a sample of disabled children, whether they were depressed was significantly affected by who their parents compared them with. Children of parents who used healthy, able-bodied children as the basis for comparing their disabled offspring's performance were more depressed than those whose parents used other disabled children as the standard. Daughters of pushy mothers tend to set themselves impossibly high standards, with the curious result that many high-achieving girls actually have lower self-esteem than their less successful sisters. One British study by West and Sweeting measured levels of anxiety and depression in two very large representative samples of fifteen-year-old children (5,000 per sample), in 1987 and again in 1999. In the lowest social class, girls' rates rose only a little, but in the top class – the group most likely to become academic high-flyers – the rise was from 24 per cent in 1987 to a startling 38 per cent in 1999. Stricter categorisation showed that major emotional distress (the kind that can require hospitalisation) had risen threefold amongst the affluent girls, from 6 per cent in 1987 to 18 per cent in 1999. The reasons the girls gave for their distress, and the explanation for the rise in it, were worries about weight, about school performance and about exams.

These findings are by no means restricted to affluent British high-achieving girls. An American study, of more than 250 upper-middle-class sixteen-year-old girls, also found three times more depression amongst them than children from low-income homes, as well as higher rates of anxiety and substance abuse (which appeared to be a form of self-medication for emotional disturbance). In another study, of 302 affluent American thirteen-year-old girls, depression was twice as high and there was further evidence of self-medicating substance abuse. Lack of closeness to parents and intense pressures to achieve predicted which girls were suffering, although it did not do so amongst boys, who, like their British peers, seemed much less likely to become preoccupied by academic perfectionism. The girls appeared to have introjected their parents' perfectionist standards and had low self-esteem for failing to meet them, love being conditional on success. Interestingly, however, having high standards for children did not predict how successful they were – pushy parenting did not work.

This pattern of findings appears to endure into young adulthood, amongst students. One study of the gravity of American students' symptoms from 1989 to 2001 showed that they had become both more severe and more complex, with a doubling in the amount of depression. Another study showed that self-esteem in students for whom it was tied to academic performance was more likely to plummet if they learnt that they had not gained entry to a desired university: self-esteem is more prone to fluctuation if tied to external goals. A study of 122 American students found that those who felt they had done badly in coursework or exams, the ones whose self-esteem was contingent on academic success, were more prone to depression and lowered self-esteem, leading to wild fluctuations in it, depending on daily victories and defeats. Whilst most students' moods were affected by bad academic news, those who did not judge their worth primarily by performance in this realm were less affected and recovered quicker. Sadly, even when those with contingent self-esteem felt they had done well, their self-esteem was not markedly improved – they dismissed success and moved straight on to the next challenge. Perhaps surprisingly, since it might be assumed that they work harder, students with contingent self-esteem were not more likely to do well. A particularly thorough study of 642 students followed their emotional vicissitudes from the start to the end of their first year at university. The ones whose self-worth depended on academic success were much more stressed than ones for whom it did not. The former group felt short of time, fell out with peers and teachers, derived little pleasure in the actual performance of the work and, however good their grades were, were less satisfied on hearing their results. Consistent with the findings of the previous studies, their grades were anyway not improved by their esteem-driven concern to do well, apparently hampered by cumulative stress and handicapped by anxiety during exams.

The final conclusion of this study is that it is having self-esteem contingent on performance that explains the poor academic performance of people with low self-esteem, rather than the low self-esteem per se. This is borne out by studies showing that methods of caring for patients or teaching pupils are more effective if they encourage autonomy rather than if they are pedagogically authoritarian. If taught in a way that fosters autonomy, pupils do better, are more focused on the satisfactions of learning, get more enjoyment and cope better with failure. Likewise, when clients trying to give up smoking or drinking or to lose weight are encouraged to be autonomous by the doctor or trainer, they succeed more. A study of medical students during their training found that if autonomy was encouraged, the students' social skills with patients were better, and the students in turn were more likely to have encouraged autonomy in the patients.

Having said all this, it is interesting to reflect that even if a considerable and increasing number of students are being damaged by performance-dominated parents and societies, there are still plenty who are academic high-achievers and undamaged. In an American study of 460 parents of twelve-year-old high-flyers, when encouraging their children, over one-third of the mothers or fathers focused on the love of learning, challenge-seeking in the work and the development of self-motivation. More than one-fifth of mothers or fathers were performance-minded: stressing grades, doing better than other students and the long-term importance of these for getting the job which would pay a high salary that they urged upon their children. There were also a minority of cases in which one or other parent stressed both performance and 'love of learning' goals. Children with a performance-minded parent were at greater risk of self-critical perfectionism, but there were still a considerable number of high-achieving children whose parents were not being controlling or fostering extrinsic values by their nurture.

Ten per cent of the 460 parents were of Asiatic ethnic origin, and in more than two-thirds of such cases one parent or the other was performance-minded. Several other studies have shown that Asian parents are far more likely to have an authoritarian parenting style and performance-minded goals, but fascinatingly, whereas that can lead to low grades if found in white families, it does not in Asian ones. This is because, although the Asian children are controlled and dominated, that is also accompanied by a great deal of warmth and loving attention. By contrast, in white performance-minded families nurture also tends to be cold and rejecting: love is conditional on success, whereas amongst Asians that is less likely.

Refinements of Kasser's analysis

Tim Kasser and colleagues have provided a scientific foundation for many of Erich Fromm's theories. They offer persuasive evidence that materialism prevents people from meeting four basic needs: security, self-esteem, good relationships and authentic experience. In accord with this, as we have seen, Kasser has provided persuasive evidence that materialists are more insecure, have lower self-esteem, have worse relationships and are more inauthentic. He proposes the extrinsic goals of the materialists as the reason they have these problems more. He concludes that we need a radical shift away from those pursuits and towards intrinsic ones if we want a society which maximises well-being, much as Erich Fromm suggested.

Three studies have questioned whether Kasser is right in asserting that extrinsic goals are the cause of misery, in and of themselves. In the first place, whilst there is little doubt that many people with extrinsic goals are more miserable, that still leaves some people with them who are not; likewise, not all seekers after intrinsic goals are happy bunnies. In 1998, Charles Carver and Eryn Baird published a study which suggested that 'it's not what you want but why you want it that matters'. They distinguished between goals and motives. Consider a Briton who went from a major public school to an Oxbridge university, got a good degree and had the contacts to waltz into a merchant bank. Now suppose that they chose instead to become a social worker. That occupation has an ostensibly intrinsic goal in that it puts helping others and making the world a better place before money. However, the reasons the person might choose this job could be essentially extrinsic: they might be seeking to make people think better of them or to avoid feelings of guilt (perhaps because of values introjected from parents and subsequent peer group). Undoubtedly, whilst probably rare, such people do exist. I can think of some very stern folk who work in universities or in the health and social services who would seem outwardly to be 'about doing good' but whose motives for doing so are essentially to get to the top of their profession in order to be admired. One university researcher I know, whilst her goals are impeccably intrinsic (to do research that will improve our well-being), has motives so shockingly extrinsic as to make the most attention-seeking of talentless celebrities seem authentic by comparison.

It is also possible to have extrinsic goals with intrinsic motives. A person might seek highly paid work because they believe it will be more fun and more challenging, and give them greater control over their destiny (in their personal as well as their professional life). Although also probably rare birds, I certainly know of some people like this. One has found his work tremendously interesting, is a model citizen in every way (contributing a great deal to his family and the community) and yet is also motivated to make his company a financial success. This suggests that it is possible to pursue simultaneously financial (extrinsic) goals for intrinsic motives, and yet to be either miserable or fulfilled. In other words, it's not as simple as 'intrinsic goals good, extrinsic goals bad', nor 'intrinsic motives good, extrinsic motives bad'.

In Carver and Baird's study, 246 students were differentiated according to whether they had extrinsic motives (to fit in with social pressures, to please parents, to gain admiration) or intrinsic ones (to have fun, to gain satisfaction, to be in control of their life). Their goals were also measured and so was their well-being. Overall, just like Kasser, they found that having (extrinsic) financial success as a goal produced lower well-being and that those who pursued (intrinsic) community involvement were happier. However, when motives were taken into account, it emerged that students who had intrinsic motives for aspiring to financial success did have well-being, and this aspiration only made them unhappy if they had extrinsic motives. The same was true once motives were factored in for community involvement: intrinsic motives for it raised well-being, extrinsic ones made you unhappy. Carver and Baird admitted that, overall, the students who pursued financial goals were liable to be unhappier than ones with community goals, so something about financial goals may militate against well-being, in and of itself. But they also concluded that having the right motive for financial aspiration could make you happy, and that having the wrong motive for community involvement could make you unhappy.

This line of thinking was taken a step further in 2001, by

Abhishek Srivastava and colleagues. Instead of undergraduates, this time the samples were 240 MBA postgraduate
students and 145 entrepreneurs, groups both likely to put
financial goals high on their list. Srivastava pointed out that
some people may pursue money as an instrumental means
for achieving personal life goals and values, even if many
others do so to gain status and generate the envy and admiration of others. They also distinguished between pursuing
money as a pathological compensation for feelings of low
self-esteem and insecurity, and doing so to express one's
healthier desires, whether the practical need to house and
feed oneself and one's family, or simply personal fulfilment.
The results showed that people have many different motives
for having money as a goal. Positive ones included meeting
basic material needs, supporting a family and self-esteem;
the negative ones were overcoming self-doubt, showing off
and gaining power. Like Kasser, Srivastava and colleagues
found that people who pursued money were unhappier, but
like Carver, that once you took motives into account it was
not the money pursuit itself that was primarily harmful, it
was the motive. As a goal it becomes problematic if you
hope that its acquisition will achieve what it cannot: things
like buying love or improving character or regaining self-
esteem. Specifically, they claim that it is harmful when it is

used as a material substitute for the life of the mind (Being rather than Having; in accord with this, a more recent study found that buying experiences, such as trekking in the Himalayas, makes people happier than buying material possessions, such as an iPod).

The third study, published in 2003 by Ariel Malka and Jennifer Chapman, explored how motivations affected job satisfaction and how this in turn affected overall well-being. One hundred and twenty-four MBA students were assessed during their degree and followed up to see how they fared four to nine years later. Malka and Chapman's basic point of departure was that, depending on how extrinsic or intrinsic the motivation, financial success – extrinsic goals – should be more or less likely to result in well-being. Extrinsic people see the main purpose of working as to make money, whereas the intrinsic see it as a source of intellectual fulfilment, self-expression and mastering of tasks. If an extrinsically motivated person gets well paid, it should make them happier – if money matters to you and you get it, you should feel tickety-boo. I know many people who make no pretence that they find their work interesting but who deliberately sought it because they wanted to be able to afford an upper-middle-class house and lifestyle (school fees, etc). For some of them, so long as the pay keeps going up, they seem reasonably satisfied, at least with their work. Intriguingly, Malka and Chapman hypothesised that not only would an intrinsically motivated person be no happier for earning more, they might actually be unhappier. This is because intrinsic motivation is satisfying to someone who prizes it only if it increases their sense of self-determination, of autonomy. Increased pay could reduce that sense, making the person feel controlled by bosses and that they are only doing it for the money, thus reducing both job and life satisfaction. Indeed, 128 studies have found that external rewards reduce intrinsic motivations. To some extent, when considering a job everyone trades off the interest of the work against the pay. Extrinsically motivated people would have already accepted higher pay over interest, so jobs which paid well but were boring would not dissatisfy them as much as the intrinsically motivated. On the contrary, it could even be that the higher the pay, the greater the intrinsically motivated person's dissatisfaction with a job which has little intrinsic value. The high earners I know who would dearly love to be able to do something interesting but feel, for all sorts of reasons, that they must put that to one side and pursue money-making occupations are often deeply unhappy, although they are not always aware of it. For some of them, a pay rise can actually have the effect of ramming home just how dissatisfied they are with their work. There may be many others who feel this way but will not admit it to themselves, let alone to others.

Malka and Chapman's results bore out most of these points. Overall, for the extrinsically motivated, the higher their pay, the happier they were and the greater their job satisfaction. For the intrinsically motivated, higher pay not only did not make them happier, it actually made them unhappier than intrinsically motivated people with lower pay. Interestingly, though, higher pay did not lead the intrinsically motivated to be more dissatisfied with their job. Malka and Chapman speculated that this could be because the intrinsically motivated could not face admitting to themselves that their mistaken decision to put money ahead of job interest had not only made them unhappy, it was boring them to existential death – perhaps they had to cling on to some reason to get up and go to work in the morning.

Needless to say, Kasser did not take these critiques lying down. In a 2004 paper, subtitled 'It's both what you pursue and why you pursue it', he pointed to various weaknesses in these three studies and disputed whether the results really did demonstrate the paramount importance of motives over goals. He then presented the results of three new studies. First off, they showed that people with extrinsic goals also usually have extrinsic motives. In other words, the sort of person who decides to become a stockbroker with the motive of making oodles of dosh also tends to be the sort of person with that goal; by implication, the person with intrinsic motivation and extrinsic goals is an exception. Next he showed that individuals with the highest well-being in his study were the ones with intrinsic goals and motives, a finding that has been replicated several times elsewhere. What was more, if intrinsic goals were good for your health, they were not as good for it as extrinsic ones were bad: extrinsic goals made you unhappier to an even greater extent than intrinsic ones made you happier. It was true, as his critics had suggested, that both goals and motives of both types independently predicted happiness levels and that financial goals alone did not. But his critics were wrong to claim that motives were more important than goals, since both were strong predictors and since they tended to go together by type (extrinsic goals with extrinsic motives, intrinsic with intrinsic). Kasser's conclusion bears quoting: 'people seeking greater well-being would be well advised to focus on the pursuit of (a) goals involving [personal] growth, [community] connection, and contribution rather than goals involving money, beauty, and popularity and (b) goals that are interesting and personally important to them rather than goals they feel forced or pressured to pursue'. In short, if you want to be happy, it is most likely to happen if you pursue intrinsic goals and motives. This may be true statistically, but it still leaves the door open for the theoretically possible case of a happy, intrinsically motivated merchant banker and for an extrinsically motivated nurse who is full of beans. It's just that there are probably not many of either type about.

These studies go to the heart of many affluent people's predicament: working for pleasure (as a vehicle for Being) versus working for money, status or power (as a vehicle for Having).

The evidence in this chapter suggests that materialism is a significant cause of emotional distress. In analysing materialism's causes, we have seen that a great many factors contribute, from television viewing habits, to kinds of schooling, to intimate relationships. Societies vary in how much they engender those patterns which encourage materialism. If a society changed from one which did not encourage it to one that did, you would expect an increase in emotional distress. That is what I believe occurred in the English-speaking world: the emergence of what I term Selfish Capitalism in the English-speaking world during the 1970s increased materialism, increasing distress.

Chapter 3
From Selfish Capitalism To Materialism To Distress

At the end of the 1970s, the governments of the USA and Britain broke with the Keynesian consensus which had dominated since the war and adopted neo-liberal policies – what was called Thatcherism and Reaganomics, and what I term Selfish Capitalism. Eventually, it prevailed in the other English-speaking nations as well. Although some Selfish Capitalist elements were adopted by some mainland Western European nations, they remained largely Unselfish. This difference, I maintain, explains why one set of countries (the English-speaking) has twice the prevalence of distress of the other (mainland Western Europe). Above all, Selfish Capitalism engenders distress through the pressure it places on citizens to be materialistic, although it distresses in many other ways as well.

Defining Selfish Capitalism

Selfish Capitalism is a form of political economy that has four defining features. The first is that the success of a company is judged largely by its current share price, rather than by its underlying strength or its contribution to the society or economy. The second is a strong drive to privatise collective goods, such as water, gas and electrical utilities. The third is minimal regulation of financial services and labour markets, including the introduction of working practices that strongly favour employers and disfavour trade unions, making it easier to hire and fire. Alongside this, taxes are not concerned with redistribution of wealth, making it easier for corporations and the rich to avoid them, and to use tax havens within the law. The fourth defining feature is the conviction that consumption and market forces can meet human needs of almost every kind.

In what follows, although I shall frequently write of Selfish Capitalism as if it has a will, seemingly anthropomorphising, it is an impersonal mechanism. Although some of its elements are centuries old, in its present form it has mutated out of advanced industrialisation. It encourages social, economic, political and cultural forms and contents that maximise it, and works against those which impede it, especially if they might improve the emotional well-being of the population. Selfish Capitalism cannot afford for us to be satisfied, for that would stifle rampant consumerism and materialist values, which are essential for its operation.

The economic and theoretical roots of Selfish Capitalism can be traced back, via Leo Strauss and Milton Friedman in the 1970s, and David Ricardo and Thomas Malthus in the nineteenth century, to Adam Smith in the eighteenth century. It has many close siblings with names like market liberalism, free-market economics, Neo-conservatism, Neo-liberalism, Reaganomics, Thatcherism. As a basic theory of political economy, it approximates most closely to Neo-liberalism. The American political scientist David Harvey describes Neo-liberalism's basic tenets as the proposition that human well-being can best be advanced by liberating individual entrepreneurial freedoms and skills within a state-provided framework characterised by strong private property rights, free markets and free trade, seeking to bring all human action into the domain of the market. At this level of abstraction, Harvey demonstrates that neo-liberalism can coexist successfully with the political Left as well as Right, so that it was adopted in modified form by Social Democratic Sweden and nominally-Communist China in the 1980s, as well as being imposed upon much of the developing world and the post-Soviet societies (through the

International Monetary Fund, World Bank and World Trade Organization), to greater or lesser degrees. Whilst a close political blood relative of Neo-conservatism, Neo-liberalism does not include as part of its definition the neo-con's rampant and all-encompassing moralism, its love of nationalism as a rallying cry or its penchant for authoritarianism.

In terms of practical political policy, the best account of the kinds of measures which tend to accompany Selfish Capitalism is known as the Washington Consensus, a list of eleven key policy commitments largely devised by American and British political economists to facilitate globalisation after 1975: the liberalisation of international financial markets; the same in domestic financial markets; trade liberalisations (especially in developing nations); labour market 'flexibility'; security of private property, financial and physical assets; weak rights over human assets (particularly skills); reduced public sector spending, for example via privatisations and making business less regulated by the state; shifting the tax burden from rich to poor and from capital assets to workers, with subsidies increasingly for capital rather than workers; independent central banks; reduced welfare provisions, such as sickness and unemployment benefits; and privatisation (to charitable or voluntary organisations) and liberalisation of social policy.

However, none of these measures, nor the tenets of neo-liberalism, capture precisely what I want to convey with the words 'Selfish Capitalism', for they refer to an underlying principle akin to the biological notion of natural selection. Nor is Selfish Capitalism the sole preserve of any form of governance, political persuasion or single nation. On top of that, in choosing the word Selfish, I hope to spell out the underlying impulse of the politics entailed, cutting to the truth behind three decades of doublethinking obfuscation ('The Third Way') and faux-science (Monetarism): it's a Look After Number One, bugger everyone else, way of organising things; selfish, in fact.

In some respects, Selfish Capitalism theory imitates Darwin's famous explanation for the evolution of species. He showed that species which prospered were chosen by natural selection, the ones that were well adapted to their current environment flourishing, and the ones that were not, eventually dying out. With the discovery of genes, the argument was elaborated: evolution occurred through random genetic mutations, some of which aid successful adaptation, which leads to increased likelihood of survival and incorporation of those mutations into the species gene pool.

Analogously, I maintain, social forms and contents will be selected by Selfish Capitalism if they support it and will disappear if they do not, a point I develop in chapter 4. In choosing the word 'selfish' to label this form of capitalism, as well as trying to be provocatively explicit about its goal, I am intentionally echoing Richard Dawkins' famous use of that word. I wish to question the extent to which the 'selfishness' of our genes should exercise us in explaining our contemporary psychology, as much as this form of capitalism. My use of the word challenges a fundamental premise of classical economic theory and much social science: that individuals will maximise their material gains at the expense of others, and expect others to do the same. Although this can be true of some people, in some circumstances, a vast body of evidence shows that we can also be altruistic: concerned with fairness and reciprocity, and ready to sacrifice gains and to punish others who do not play fair. Most crucially, what kind of society, and family within it, that a person is from hugely affects how selfish or unselfish they are as individuals.

I use the term 'Unselfish Capitalism' to denote a capitalism which limits personal profits and fosters personal well-being. The epitome of Selfish Capitalism is the USA and Denmark is its opposite. Both government and business in the English-speaking world prior to the 1970s approximated more closely to Unselfish Capitalism. After the Second

World War egalitarianism, meritocracy, social mobility and, arguably above all, the mass media began to spread materialism to the masses as well as the elites, by encouraging everyone to aspire to anything. The spread did not occur immediately. It was not until the Sixties that traditional class hierarchy and patriarchy began their rapid demise. There had been considerable privation during the war, so that a growing desire for money and possessions (but not yet the yearning for fame or universal obsession with appearance) in the 'you've never had it so good' Fifties was an extension of wartime survival materialism, rather than the relative variety. Until the Seventies, developed nations were becoming increasingly equal, with very substantial proportions of the poor and of women gaining access to unprecedented incomes, as well as freedoms. Both government and business still regarded the emotional well-being of the population as important, reinvesting much higher proportions of profits in business innovation and social welfare.

By contrast, substantial economic inequality is among the most significant of the many consequences of Selfish Capitalism. It demands rapid and substantial returns on capital in the name of shareholder value. Executives take share options in public companies as an incentive to increase the value of shares, although it is highly questionable whether this is actually the outcome. What does happen is that wealth rapidly concentrates in a few hands. Companies become commodities to be bought and sold in a turmoil of takeover, merger and demerger. Manufacturing is rapidly replaced by financial and other services as drivers of the economy. Job insecurity becomes widespread as employers impose short-term contracts and demand 'flexible' working. Saving is replaced by debt. Marketing and advertising become a larger proportion of GDP as companies go for quick fixes to sell products, in order to jack up the share price (although, again, it is doubtful that this is actually what is achieved).

Why did Selfish Capitalism spread so widely after the 1970s?

Like many other people, my eyes tend to glaze over when I read accounts of the increase in the wealth of the rich in the last thirty years but, just for a moment, I would plead with the reader to resist this reaction and, also, to put their political beliefs to one side. Try to read closely and to think about the following facts, familiar though the territory may be:

- Taxes for the wealthiest people have dropped very sharply since the 1970s.

- In Britain, the top 1 per cent of income earners in Britain has doubled its share of the national income from 6.5 per cent to 13 per cent since 1982.

- Internationally, the income gap between the bottom one-fifth richest countries and the top one-fifth richest changed from 1:30 in 1960, to 1:60 in 1990, to 1:74 in 1997.

- The world's richest 200 people more than doubled their net worth in just the four years between 1994 and 1998 to more than $1 trillion.

Now consider these less often mentioned facts:

- Real wages (adjusted for inflation) have either decreased or remained static in the USA and Britain since the 1970s. For example, the post-war peak in the USA was $15.72 per hour, falling to $14.15 in 2000, even though productivity was constantly rising.

- The growth in average household income that has occurred in the last thirty years has been achieved in two main ways in the Selfish Capitalist world:

1. By women becoming as likely as men to have paid employment (ie average income has not increased, getting women into the workforce to create dual income households is what has raised overall affluence).

2. Working hours have substantially increased for the average household, especially the average professional or managerial worker.

- The ultimate justification of Selfish Capitalism is that it promotes general well-being by promoting economic growth, yet it is now accepted by many economists that its sole reliable achievement is to have reduced inflation. It is a myth that Selfish Capitalism is more successful, economically. Despite having been systematically disseminated to many parts of the globe since the early 1980s (albeit with patchy implementation), global annual rates of economic growth were highest in the Keynesian 1960s (3.5 per cent) and 1970s (2.4 per cent), lowest in the Selfish Capitalist 1980s (1.4 per cent) and 1990s (1.1 per cent).

It is an undeniable fact that the rich have got a very great deal richer under Selfish Capitalism. A recent analysis of income distributions, internationally and over time, has shown that the proportion of wealth owned by the very richest has increased substantially in English-speaking nations since the 1970s, compared with mainland Western Europe. Those in the top 0.1 per cent of incomes in the USA went from earning 2 per cent of total income share to over 7 per cent. In Britain, the increase was from the same base to nearly 4 per cent; in Canada it rose to 5 per cent. By contrast, for example in France (and Japan), the proportion remained the same, at 2 per cent.

Of course, in a longer historical perspective, these disparities are still nowhere near as high as in 1913, where the top 0.1 per cent of earners in Canada, Britain and the USA garnered 8 to 12 per cent of all income. But their incomes declined steadily from 1914 onwards, reduced by two world wars and the subsequent shift towards social democratic politics. For thirty years after 1945 in the USA and UK, relatively Unselfish Capitalism held sway. In the USA, between 1941 and 1950 the income of the lowest fifth of families increased by 42 per cent, whereas the highest fifth's actually fell (by 2 per cent). The large inequalities following the introduction of Selfish Capitalism mean it has been decades since the real income of the majority of Americans has increased, and since the 1970s only the top

fifth have seen theirs increase. It is also undeniable that the
rest of the population have had to work harder for less or no
increased reward.

Although much more debatable than these facts, there is
a strong case that Selfish Capitalism came into being when
it did for one very simple reason: the rich were getting
poorer and they wished to re-establish their wealth. David
Harvey sets the scene for this scenario, as follows: after the
Second World War 'the economic power of the upper classes
was restrained and labour accorded a much larger share of
the economic pie. In the USA, for example, the share of the
national income taken by the top 1 per cent of income earners fell from a pre-war high of 16 per cent to less than 8 per
cent by the end of the war and stayed close to that level for
nearly three decades. While growth was strong this restraint
seemed not to matter. To have a stable share of an increasing pie is one thing but when growth collapsed in the 1970s,
when real interest rates went negative and paltry dividends
and profits were the norm, then upper classes everywhere
felt threatened. In the US the control of wealth (as opposed
to income) by the top 1 per cent of the population had
remained fairly stable throughout the twentieth century. But
in the 1970s it plunged precipitously as asset values (stocks,
property, savings) collapsed. The upper classes had to move

decisively if they were to protect themselves from political and economic annihilation.' Harvey goes on to provide persuasive evidence for his account of what happened next.

Realising that their position was threatened, the wealthy elite teamed up to create consent for the re-establishment of their position. American businesses joined federations, 'boss unions' like the American Chamber of Commerce (its membership grew from 60,000 firms in 1972 to 250,000 in 1982). The explicit intention of the leaders of this movement was to influence government, the academic world and the media. An organisation of CEOs called the Business Roundtable declared itself 'committed to the aggressive pursuit of political power for the corporation'. The corporations involved amassed a huge war chest and began spending $900 million annually on achieving influence, a vast sum in the 1970s. Not all was spent on buying politicians: considerable amounts were also used to set up think tanks with authoritative-sounding names, like the Heritage Foundation and the American Enterprise Institute (in the UK in the Seventies came the Institute of Economic Affairs and the Centre for Policy Studies). American academia being already privatised, it was a relatively simple matter to pay academics to do serious economic and socio-political scientific studies which supported Selfish Capitalist tenets. Before long, the likes of Milton Friedman were becoming highly influential in economics departments and business schools, institutions which were used to train the next leaders of the developing world. This was to prove very helpful in the coming decades in persuading them to take out huge loans from the IMF and World Bank.

At the same time, it was a simple matter for business to disseminate Selfish Capitalist thinking. Providing campaign funds for politicians who already thought that way was straightforward. Equally, since the vast majority of newspapers and television companies, and, subsequently, of publishing houses, were owned or soon to be owned by Selfish Capitalist moguls, it was hardly difficult to ensure that the public were told the 'right' story. Of course, many of the politicians, journalists, academics and authors who told it did sincerely believe their own rhetoric. They honestly believed that they were 'setting the people free' by deregulating business and financial services, disempowering unions, reducing tax for the wealthy, and in reducing state expenditure on health, education, public housing, pensions and social welfare. The meritocratic rhetoric of the post-war consensus was employed: Selfish Capitalism would allow the individual to flourish, it would permit upward social mobility for those with talent, it would allow women, immigrants, and eventually even homosexuals (in the UK the likes of Tories such as Matthew Parris and Alan Duncan could be outed without suffering) to realise their true potentialities. There is no doubt that the thinkers and politicians who espoused these ideals believed these outcomes would be the consequences of their policies. Making the rich richer was not their primary intention.

In the UK, for example, there is little question of the sincerity of Margaret Thatcher or Keith Joseph that neo-liberalism would fulfil these ideals, likewise the journalists and other fellow-travellers, academic or social policy minded. The policies would raise the wealth of all, creating a trickle-down effect. It is only very recently that it has finally become accepted by almost all serious economists that the evidence shows that the very opposite is what happens – a flood of wealth upwards – so that, whatever your political convictions, it is an undeniable fact that Selfish Capitalism robs the poor to give to the rich. That may not be the intention of its adherents, some of whom may even regard it as a regrettable by-product, but it is undeniable.

Whether senior figures in British or American corporations, or in the world of finance, felt this as sincerely or passionately is more doubtful. They were very confident that such policies would lead to much greater personal wealth for themselves and most probably, if sympathetic politicians and members of the intelligentsia told them in speeches, books and newspaper articles that this would be for the good of all, then they were happy to believe it, assuming they gave it any thought at all. As for the old rich, as they read about Thatcher's ideas in their newspapers, they could feel nothing but relief on hearing them, whilst quite possibly sincerely believing it would be best for the nation as well as their bank balances.

But as David Harvey meticulously maps out, it was soon apparent that once Selfish Capitalism was implemented, it was very far from being for the common good. Taking the example of New York City, he shows how the cutting of public services and destruction of public goods rapidly led to a broken society (in speaking of mending it, David Cameron, the current British Conservative leader, shows no sign of realising that, without Unselfish Capitalism, no amount of talk about strengthening the family will help). Neo-conservatism from politicians soon filled the social void, with promises to get tough backed by flamboyant moralising, toxic nationalism and racism, and what was true of New York was true for the rest of the USA and the UK. The Selfish Capitalism of the 1980s brought high unemployment, high inflation at the end of the decade, lower wages for harder work, and the mantra that it was up to the individual to take responsibility for failure, as the 'liberated' individual was increasingly made to pay for services on an individual basis. When the social glue came unstuck, Reagan and Thatcher responded with highfaluting neo-con rhetoric to justify the armed suppression of rioting masses in Los Angeles and Liverpool. But above all, from the standpoint of the general economic good, the success stories of the 1980s were not the UK or the USA but West Germany and Japan – except, that is, for the top 1 per cent of Britons and Americans, whose wealth massively expanded.

There were considerable disparities between the rhetoric of what neo-liberalism was supposed to be achieving and what actually occurred. In the 1950s and 1960s, American industry had become highly innovative and productive, with profits reinvested into research and development. Although rarely alluded to by influential free-market thinkers such as Milton Friedman and Leo Strauss, private industry in the USA received (and receives) a great deal of government subsidy. The massive sums spent by the government on defence led to technologies which were then exploited for commercial gain. The B-52 bomber became the basis for Boeing's domination of the global aircraft industry. IBM computers emerged from the Second World War air defence system. The semiconductor industry was founded on huge government orders. Goods and services purchased by the US Government had to be from American firms, and even today, although the myth of a free market is promulgated, the government still provides substantial support for various industries, both directly through subsidies (President Bush's energy policy bill provided $2.9 billion to the coal industry, $4.3 billion to nuclear power and $1.5 billion to oil and gas firms) and indirectly through protectionism (such as, currently, a 25 per cent import tax on steel). On top of that, where there are public-private partnerships, the taxpayer usually takes all or most of the risk, the private company getting virtually guaranteed profits. Although the Selfish Capitalist ideology loudly proclaims the need for individuals to be self-supporting, oddly enough, when the rich come unstuck the state leaps to their rescue. Only this year the Federal Reserve came galloping along with billions of dollars to bail out the banks following the subprime mortgage problems. It was the same story in the 1980s when junk bonds went belly up.

More fundamentally, Selfish Capitalist economies have a tendency to be built on debt and thin air, rather than truly productive infrastructures. According to the economic journalist Will Hutton, the flourishing, innovative post-war

American economy was weakened by economics that prioritised profit for shareholders and business executives obsessed with financial engineering, which prevented reinvestment and innovation. The new creed contended that tax was an unfair burden on the citizen. It was characterised as the state stealing from the individual what was rightfully theirs, inhibiting and distorting business, and providing welfare support (health and social services) for the poor or disadvantaged which removed their sense of responsibility. Businesses were held to have no duty to the community: it was up to rich private individuals if they wanted to provide money through charitable donations for such things as education or health care for people in the wider society. Rather than being judged by their innovation and long-term growth, the principal arbiter of a company's success became its current share price. Very rapid and large returns were demanded by investors. Increasingly, the businesses themselves were perceived as commodities, no different from the goods and services they produced, to be bought and sold for the profit of senior managers and financial middlemen, such as merchant bankers.

There was a profound change in executives' remuneration. They began to demand share options as a personal incentive to run the business, getting them to focus on its share price. Profit reporting became short-term, quarterly rather than annual. As recently as 1990, only 2 per cent of US traded shares belonged to company directors in the form of share options, but by 2001 this had risen to 13 per cent. However, following the temporary fall in share prices in the early years of this century, executives increasingly demanded money up front as well as share options. Huge salary packages, such as Michael Eisner's $200 million a year when he was CEO at Disney, became commoner and were usually unrelated to the actual performance of the company, the excuse given for massive payouts. By 2001 there were 4,000 executives on Wall Street earning more than a million dollars a year, and the average salary of the chief executives of the top 362 companies was $12.4 million, six times higher than that in 1990, five hundred times the average income. Financial engineering became a crucial skill for a chief executive. Buying other companies and gutting them was one way to boost your own company's share price. Loss-making sections were sold first, then workforces were reduced in size – as was their pay – and the filleted company could be sold on at a profit. Another method was 'creative accounting', famously ending in disaster in the case of Enron.

The changes made since the 1970s have made a mockery of the fabled American Dream. Today, the USA's poor are

less likely to exit from poverty than those of Canada,
Britain, Sweden, the Netherlands and Germany. If they do
manage it, they are more likely to have returned to poverty
five years later. A white-skinned American male today is no
more likely to be upwardly socially mobile than he was in
1950. Access to wealth through education is largely down to
family background: a 1965 study showed that two-thirds of
educational performance was explicable by background,
and the same was true in 1995. In 1979, students whose
families were from the top one-quarter of earners were four
times as likely to obtain a university degree than students
from the bottom quarter; now they are nine times as likely
to. Definitive analysis of the causes of performance on the
national Standard Assessment Tests (SATs) proved the large
extent to which they measure middle-classness, rather than
ability. These facts caused 120 American billionaires to
campaign against Bush's tax cuts for the rich in 2001
because they feared that a new aristocracy was being created
which would ultimately damage the nation's productivity, by
ensuring that only an increasingly in-bred, dim-witted elite
would become the leaders of the future. When President
Bush Jr claimed that 'We are the brightest beacons for freedom and opportunity in the world,' or when a senior politician said that 'Americans should not deny the fact that of all

the nations in the history of the world theirs is the most just, the most tolerant and the best model for the future,' they were either lying or oblivious of the real facts.

In Britain after 1978, something very similar occurred. Thatcherism drew heavily upon US market liberalism for its inspiration. She said, 'The fundamental strength of the American economy is the underlying enterprise culture of the American people. It is therefore vital to secure in this country [Britain} that same enterprise culture.' To impose American capitalism on us, despite the findings of surveys revealing our continued European tendency to see ourselves as social animals and our belief in the need to redistribute wealth, she created a 'flexible' workforce (removing workers' rights), privatised nationalised industries as much as was politically possible, cut taxes on the rich, shrank welfare support for the poor, deregulated business and offered state support for entrepreneurs. Manufacturing declined rapidly; the proportion of the workforce employed in financial services went from 10 per cent to 19 per cent; jobs became gender-neutral and on short contracts. The results were, to say the least, mixed as far as the general good was concerned. Paralysis of business by unions was largely eradicated, inflation fell (although not as a result of monetarism) but unemployment and inequality mushroomed.

Whilst it was an astonishing feat of political dexterity and determination to have achieved such radical change, it should not be forgotten that, in the process, Thatcher effectively donated vast quantities of her citizens' resources to a tiny handful. In pricing the nationalised assets to avoid the risk of the sales not being popular, she offered them for much less than their true value, most conspicuously so in the case of council houses (be sure to read Florio's book *The Great Divestiture* if you do not believe this). Investors in deprivatised industries achieved huge windfalls, overnight, their shares increasing in value by one-quarter to four-fifths. Instead of reinvesting the profits from these sales in infrastructure, Thatcher used them to fund tax cuts. And what is often forgotten is that this was the period of peak income from North Sea oil and gas revenues, with an average of £8 billion coming in every year. A never-to-be-repeated opportunity to invest in infrastructure was lost (cf Norway, which created a national trust fund for its oil and gas revenues now worth £107 billion), and instead the plague of problems which accompany Selfish Capitalism was visited upon us: child poverty (up from 19 per cent of all children in 1979 to 31 per cent in 1981, staying there for the rest of the Tory era), much greater income inequality, reduced reinvestment in industry, short-term concern with returns on shares, and stagnating public services (rail, health, welfare), to name but a few. The Americanisation of Airstrip One (Orwell's name for Britain in his novel *Nineteen Eighty-Four*) was structural, from the ownership of all our major merchant banks to almost total dominance of our film distribution (so that we have to sit through movies in which British feats are depicted as American, and Brit characters as sinister or twisted) to the buying up of our utilities (disastrously so in the case of Wessex Water, which was owned by Enron and had to be bailed out by the UK Government). Whilst there were important differences, it is broadly accurate to equate American market liberalism with Thatcherism.

After eighteen years of this, in 1997, it was widely hoped that a new political era had dawned. Although the *Things Can Only Get Better* anthem which played in the background of Labour's election win seemed incontrovertible at the time, quite a few things proceeded to get a good deal worse. Complaints vary, from the Iraq war, to student fees, to the bans on fox hunting and smoking, to the fact that the rich have got considerably richer. For public-spirited people, whether or not they bought into the neo-liberal ideology of trickle-down effects and individual freedom, the biggest one is that 1997 was the moment to start repairing the damage done to the collective good in the previous eighteen years.

Instead, under the pretext of learning from the political past, Labour waited two years before deviating at all from the spending plans laid out by Major's Tory government, and since then has slavishly adhered to Selfish Capitalism. It is now pretty clear that there was no electoral need for Tony Blair's 'second-class mind' (as Roy Jenkins sneered) at all, that if John Smith had lived or if Gordon Brown had emerged from the famous Islington Granita restaurant lunch as leader, they would also have won a huge victory in 1997, and subsequently almost certainly have won at least a second term of office. Nor was it necessary to cravenly seek the support of Lord Rothermere and Rupert Murdoch. It was assumed that Labour was only conning these media magnates with comically butch, gung-ho criminal policies and claims of being the party of business, but it turns out that the real con was performed on the electorate: economically, Tony Blair is truly Thatcherite. What is more, Gordon Brown really does feel at home with American economic policies (literally as well as figuratively – for several decades, he has rented a house in Florida for his summer holidays).

Anyone who believed that Brown would undergo a radical change on ascending to the leadership would have forgotten that he has said, 'In the 1980s Margaret Thatcher rightly emphasised the importance of the enterprise culture, but this did not go far enough'. They would have been surprised to find him seeking out a photo opportunity with the Baroness not long after his ascent to power. Like the rest of the UK's ruling elite, he appears either to have swallowed the notion that taxing the rich is a mistake rather than the crucial social glue it is regarded as in the rest of Europe (in Denmark, for example, they say, 'I pay a lot of tax but I must do so in return for a great many crucial services, on which I rely') or to have convinced himself that the electorate would not stand for it. He has also bought into the incorrect dictum 'privatised efficient, nationalised inefficient', somehow ignoring the plentiful evidence to the contrary – Enron, Worldcom, GEC, the failed computerisation of public services inflicted on government departments by Accenture and other private companies. In the first five years of his chancellorship the average chief executive's salary doubled, and in the last five years the liquid assets (cash, or property that could be quickly turned into cash) of the wealthiest increased by 79 per cent. The richest 0.3 per cent now own half of the UK's liquid assets. Brown has done nothing significant to prevent the rich from using tax havens to hang on to these huge sums and pass them on to their descendants. The revelations of the role of business in funding both our main political parties completes the Americanised picture.

There has been some rearranging of the deckchairs on the *Titanic*, chronicled by New Labour's journalistic fellow-travellers perhaps to persuade themselves, as much as us, that they were not conned. Health and education spending truly have been substantially increased in a bid to repair the ailing infrastructure and to bring pay for public service workers back up from the levels to which it was deliberately allowed to drop by the Tories. However, too much of this money has been wasted on attempts to semi-privatise these services. The proportion of health money spent on administration has risen considerably, because it is so complex to combine public and private in this way. In pursuing his Private Finance Initiatives, Brown handed over ownership of publicly owned properties to private companies, as well as paying over the odds for new hospitals with fewer beds. He continued the Tory habit of flogging off school playing fields with abandon. It is true that a minimum wage had been introduced and that it kept pace with inflation, but it was a bare minimum. The tax credit system for poor people also offered help that it is unlikely a Tory government would have provided, although it has been heavily criticised for its inefficient implementation – millions of low-paid or unemployed people found them-selves under pressure to return overpayments. Arguably, the most substantial advance has been to lift 600,000 children out of poverty, but even this has been a mixed blessing. In his son-of-the-manse way, Brown seems to believe that it is only through paid work that mothers of small children can find salvation, so the Sure Start scheme for poor parents has largely turned into day-care provision, encouraging mothers to leave their children to be cared for by other women, usually poor and poorly trained, and in group care, which is often harmful. The rich can hardly be said to be quaking in their boots at the prospect of Prime Minister Brown. According to a recent paper prepared for the Citigroup Bank, the rich are now the dominant drivers of demand in English-speaking nations and this is very likely to continue to be so in the foreseeable future.

As David Harvey repeatedly points out, in all the debate about the rights and wrongs of neo-liberalism or Selfish Capitalism, this latter single fact is almost invariably ignored: that these forms of governance make the rich richer, and that may be why they have been so successful. They have demonstrably not been successful in their declared aim of promoting general well-being by promoting generally increased wealth – all the rise in affluence occurred from getting women out to work and from imposing longer hours with more insecure working conditions. Always, everywhere implemented, Selfish Capitalism coincides with massive increases in the wealth of the top 1 per cent. That makes it highly attractive to the elites who run countries and is the principal reason it flourished. The only problem was how to sell the idea to the masses and in Thatcher and Reagan, two first-class salespeople emerged. But as I shall argue in chapter 4, Selfish Capitalism also has a self-sustaining capacity to automatically attack anything which threatens it and support that which sustains it.

Whether or not David Harvey is correct in claiming that corporate America were aware that neo-liberalism would restore wealth to the wealthiest, there is no doubt that this was the consequence. It seems reasonable to suppose that the creed could be made to appeal to the ruling elites of most countries, since they would be the beneficiaries. But what is most striking is the gap between what neo-liberalism promised and what actually happened. As we shall see in the last part of this chapter, there is plausible evidence that Selfish Capitalism caused a substantial rise in distress in the English-speaking world. But before we come to that, we need to look more closely at what it is about the system that has this effect.

How Selfish Capitalism engendered distress in the USA and UK

The central contention of this book is that Selfish Capitalism creates ill-being, indeed, worse still, that discontent and misery are essential for its smooth functioning. They promote the needy consumerism which means goods are constantly being replaced by 'better' models, enabling the ever-growing short-term profits on which the system hinges. Unmaterialistic citizens, satisfied by their existing possessions and only concerned with meeting real needs, could result in nil national and corporate economic growth, or even, in contracting economies. This is not to question capitalism as such, merely the Selfish variety. The Unselfish Capitalist nations also need economic growth, but they function on a much longer timescale with the well-being of citizens placed ahead of short-term profits and rapid growth.

What happened in the USA and UK after the 1970s is a test case of the way in which Selfish Capitalism engenders distress. The single most significant change was a massive transfer of wealth and income from the state to the private sphere, and from the average person to the richest. These changes increased distress in several different ways.

In terms of survival materialism, it is true that, even in the USA, there are very few people who need actually starve. For the most part, throughout the English-speaking world, homelessness is technically a choice rather than enforced, since either charities or state-funded providers offer a bed for the night. Although the safety nets have become very threadbare compared with the 1970s, it is still the case that in the event of an emergency, fundamental physical needs – at least for food and shelter, if not for medical care – will be met for almost everyone in the English-speaking world. Far greater as a cause of distress is the relative materialism which such an unequal society generates when it is combined with the processes described in chapter 2. This is a critical point. As noted above, there were three times greater inequalities between richest and poorest at the end of the nineteenth century in the USA but it is unlikely that the distress was anything like as great then as it is now. The same is true in many developing nations – huge disparities in wealth in countries like Nigeria, yet very low prevalence of distress. What does the damage is the combination of inequality with widespread relative materialism, and that comes from Selfish Capitalism stoking up both aspirations and the expectation that they can be fulfilled. In the Big Brother society, great swathes of the population believe they, too, can be famous. In the entrepreneurial fantasy society, the delusion is fostered that anyone can be Alan Sugar or Bill Gates, never mind that the actual likelihood of this occurring has diminished since the 1970s – a person born in 1958 was more likely than one born in 1970 to achieve upward mobility through education, for example. The Selfish

Capitalist toxins that are most poisonous to well-being are the systematic encouragement of the ideas that material affluence is the key to fulfilment, that only the affluent are winners and that access to the top is open to anyone willing to work hard enough, regardless of their familial, ethnic or social class background – if you do not succeed, there is only one person to blame.

As we saw in chapter 2, these values corrode well-being but on top of that, the individual is cut adrift on a practical level, for working conditions are substantially worse under Selfish compared with Unselfish Capitalism. A study of sixteen developed nations provides convincing evidence of this, as well as demonstrating key causes of the inequalities that have opened up in the USA and UK: decline in the power of unions and decline in unconditional entitlement to services, such as welfare or housing, resulting from privatisation. In a ranking of nations according to how good their legislation is at protecting employees in the matter of hiring and firing, employers are found to have the freest hand in Singapore (123rd in how much regulation it has), then the USA (122nd), with the UK (117th), New Zealand (115th) and Australia (105th) not far behind. It is far harder for employers to do as they please in mainland Europe (eg Spain is ranked 12th, Italy 43rd and the Netherlands 60th). The differences in unconditional entitlements to public services are striking between the English-speaking nations and those of mainland Western Europe, where 50 per cent more is spent, per capita, by their governments on welfare and health. They regard the state as providing much more than a safety net. It is also there to regulate business and to ensure that everyone has the right to participate in the economy and society on an equal basis. This is reflected in the beliefs of its citizens – even British ones, despite twenty-five years of Neo-conning. Whereas 63 per cent of Britons believe that there should be redistribution of wealth through taxes, only 28 per cent of Americans do. In Europe, on average, half the citizens believe that the state should provide a basic income to people without a job, whereas only 12 per cent of Americans believe this. Remarkably, only 33 per cent of poor Americans (compared with two-thirds of Europeans) think that the state should support them.

In English-speaking countries from the 1970s onwards, there were large increases in working hours and declining job satisfaction, a reversal that did not occur in mainland Western Europe. For example, in a sample of 1,200 Britons in 2007, two-thirds said they are 'unfulfilled', 'miserable' or 'drifting' in their jobs, and over half (52 per cent) claim they'd happily earn less money in a role that made them feel better about themselves, much more than in the 1970s. In real terms there was no rise in income for American male middle- and lower-income workers between 1970 and 1995. Indeed, incomes stagnated for the majority of Americans, and in order to sustain a 'sufficient' consumer lifestyle, wives began to work as well as husbands. In 1968, families with children had a combined 53-hour average working week; by 2000 this was 64 hours. Families living on a dual income earned 60 per cent more than those with a single male earner. Americans were having to pedal faster to stay in the same consumer place. In both the UK and the USA, there was a steady growth in gender-neutral, service-industry short-term jobs, every bit as stultifying, albeit less dangerous, than the lost manufacturing ones. Job security decreased, with shorter contracts, and the proportion of people working unsocial hours (at night and weekends) rose to 15 per cent of the British workforce as shopping became almost a 24/7 activity.

Just as these lamentable changes in working conditions were happening, status competition for consumer goods was accelerating. For some time it had been 'essential' to possess a telephone, washing machine and car, but now the range of goods regarded as being in this category expanded. The prices of these 'new essentials' soon dropped, but immediately along came 'better' models which cost more but were socially imperative. The consumption patterns of the rich raised the standards of the professional and managerial classes, which raised the gate for those beneath, and so on.

Advertising played an important role in piling on this pressure. The USA has spent 2 per cent or more of its gross national product on advertising since 1968. Britain has spent 1 per cent, and likewise other English-speaking countries. By contrast, most mainland West European nations spend considerably less, around the 0.5 per cent mark. This became especially important in creating a massive personal debt burden when the financial services industry was deregulated. After 1980, personal saving plummeted in the English-speaking nations. Deregulated retail lending and liberalised mortgage-selling meant that almost the whole population were living on the never-never, exhorted to do so by hedonistic messages advertising the pleasures of consumption. By 2000, American households saved little more than zero. Personal bankruptcies in the USA rose nearly sixfold between 1980 and 2002 (from 2.5 per 1,000 households between 1960 and 1980, to 7 per 1,000 in 1990, to 14 per 1,000 in 2002). Similar patterns occurred in the UK, whereas mainland West Europeans continued to save at a high level – despite their more secure welfare safety net.

Part of this change entailed housing costs accounting for
a much higher proportion of household expenditure in the
UK and the USA. The liberalised mortgage market and, in
Britain, the sale of council houses, encouraged home ownership, with low interest rates pushing up prices. Increasingly,
single-earning families and newcomers to the market could
not get a foot on the housing ladder without borrowing far
beyond their means, resulting in the subprime mortgage
lending crisis in the USA. The market also became more
volatile, fuelling bankruptcies. In 'hot spots' such as London
and New York, the coincidence of the liberalisation of financial services, and the increase in employment therein and
salaries therefrom, created a cascade of unaffordability. In
the 1990s more than half of all new UK households were
unable to buy a house, and in London that proportion was
four-fifths. Affordable rented properties became scarcer for
low-income people as public housing was sold off. This was
particularly savage because it came at just the point in the
post-war era when incomes for the majority of English-
speaking peoples had stagnated, increasing the pressure for
dual-income earning households. Far from the leisure society predicted in the 1960s, society became workaholic.

The physical as well as the mental health of many
Britons and Americans suffered grievously, partly reflecting

the growing inequalities. In Britain, this was the result of the low spending on health by government until New Labour was elected, compared with mainland Western Europe. But even when Blair and Brown did start spending heavily on health, too much of the money was eaten up by the use of private-public initiatives. For the period 1972–76, an average unskilled British male lived 5.5 years less than a professional one. By 2002, the unskilled were living 9.5 years less. Workers with low incomes had always lived shorter lives, but after the 1970s this trend simply got worse and what was more, the proportion of the population on a low income greatly increased. In terms of life expectancy, the USA is 28th in the world league table, well below Israel or Greece, even lagging behind Costa Rica, despite being one of the wealthiest nations. Interestingly, this has little or nothing to do with the amount of money spent on health care. In 2000 the USA was the highest spender on health care per head of population, yet it came 15th in the healthiness league table of nations.

Of the many background factors, overeating was significant. Between the 1970s and 2000, the proportion of overweight American men rose from 51 to 67 per cent, and of women, from 41 to 62 per cent, with British trends following not far behind. In 2000, one-fifth of Britons and one-quarter of Americans were clinically obese. Today, one-quarter of British children are obese, putting them at increased risk of diabetes, heart problems and eventually an early grave. Ironically, but probably not coincidentally, these increases happened just when the Thin Standard, the socially accepted ideal for weight, was getting thinner. As noted in chapter 2, Britons and Americans alike were being bombarded by unprecedented quantities of media messages (not just advertisements, but in film and television as well) featuring increasingly scrawny models of 'perfection'. Such pressures have been shown many times over to increase anxiety and depression, and a very common solace when distressed in these ways is highly calorific fast food. Selfish Capitalism automatically seems to select the shortest path to the largest profit. This became visible in the waistlines of citizens as well as in their declining health and emotional well-being.

Most damaging of all to well-being, domestic and personal life were increasingly encroached upon by the market, women being placed in a particularly uncomfortable position. On the one hand, they were becoming increasingly able to obtain satisfying, well-paid work (because they were now more likely to be well educated). But on the other, materialistic competition intensified with growing dual-income household wealth. Children demanded greater investment, whether small costs, like ever-trendier trainers and mobile phones, or larger ones, like fees for the most sought-after schools or the cost of housing in the catchment areas of prized state schools. From the 1970s, husbands' incomes stagnated, jobs were more insecure and the welfare net contracted, yet all other kinds of consumerism were accelerating as well. One solution for middle-class women was to reduce the number of offspring, investing more heavily in a few. The middle-class fertility rate declined, and their families grew smaller. The other solution was to go back to work.

It was in 1982 that the number of dual-income American couples overtook single-earner ones. House prices and housing costs were driven up by the resultant increase in joint income, and the consumption hurdle over which a middle-class person must jump in order to have a 'basic' quantity and quality of status-indicating goods rose. For the American middle classes, putting their contracting number of offspring through university was a critical investment, yet in an era of stagnating incomes, fees for this vital ingredient in status success were increasing by 3 to 5 per cent a year. As the economic historian Avner Offer points out, by *choosing* to work, individually, middle-class mothers found themselves putting pressure on one another to do so, by raising

the standard of what was 'enough'. Collectively, these pressures then *compelled* mothers to work.

By the 1990s, nearly all American women completed
secondary schooling. This enabled them to compete for
better-paid, more interesting work, and that was winning
out over producing and raising children as a desirable
activity. The same status pressures that had squeezed the
middle-class mothers out of the home were now felt in families with incomes just below them. In order to keep up with
one another, the low-income manual workers' wives had to
go out to work in part-time, low-paid jobs. Now a large
proportion of the population were caught in the trap.

Avner Offer summarises the problem as having been that
the household economy became tilted against female investment in the home. The costs of marriage and staying at
home to look after children outweighed the benefits, especially amongst the best educated. Financially, the lifetime
cost of exchanging their well-paid professional work for
looking after two children was equivalent to the price of a
decent middle-class house. As noted above, dual-earner
couples' combined incomes were 60 per cent higher than
that of a single male earner. The cost of dropping out of the
market was also inflated for the well educated as their
numbers increased because one-third of Americans now had

both a degree and a professional or managerial post – too many well-educated people chasing too few jobs. As status consumption grew, the need to work increased, but the more women who did so, the higher the consumption standard rose and the more competitive the workplace became, driving up the number of hours a professional woman needed to work in order to succeed. Men also responded to the greater competition by working longer hours and professions like the law started to bill by the hour. As early as 1988, university-educated men were putting in 25 per cent more hours than those educated only to high-school level or below. At a time when mainland Europeans of both sexes were converting their greater affluence into more leisure time, Americans felt time-starved. Increasingly, even the highest-achieving women began to compromise on their careers. Two-thirds of 1970s women graduates from Harvard in law, medicine and business reported having reduced their hours at work after having children and half said that they had changed jobs to be able to do so. Increasingly, and ironically, they reported themselves dissatisfied with their work and came to look upon home as a haven from it.

Another factor tilting the balance of the emotional economy in the household was the distribution of housework. Before the 1980s, motherhood had been paid for in hard, unglamorous cleaning, nappy-changing, shopping and odd jobs. Men could not give birth and were much less inclined to take on the role of 'mother'. The arrival of a small child in the house called for two-and-a-half hours of such work each day, work that non-mothers did not have to do. Whilst fathers also increased their domestic work rate after the arrival of children, they did so by much less. Interestingly, in households of lesbians where one stayed home as mother, and in homes in which the man earned less than the woman but both worked, the mother still did the lion's share. In wealthy homes, a burgeoning immigrant workforce was employed to take up the slack, but not everyone could afford a Philippino or Polish helper.

As marriage and motherhood became less and less appealing, divorce or singledom became more so. Women, especially the well educated, began to put off marrying until their late twenties or their thirties. Cohabitation became normal for women in their twenties (with half of such rela- tionships either ending in marriage or lasting more than four years). The high-achieving childless woman found herself in a bind that was increasingly difficult to resolve as she aged.

Most were looking for an older man of similar or supe- rior background (class and education), yet the pool of such males rapidly dried up as the women got older. For one thing,

by the 1980s in the USA and the 1990s in the UK, there were
as many women as men at university, so the stock of potential eligible high-achieving mates was greatly reduced, both
there and subsequently in the workplace, as women began to
occupy prestigious jobs once largely restricted to men. For
another, men continued to prize nubility in women, and
although some women as they grew older succeeded in looking younger than previous generations had, the older
they were when seeking a reproductive partner, the more they
were disadvantaged compared to younger ones. On top of all
that, there was an actual disparity in the ratio of men to
women in the marriage market caused by the post-war baby
boom. Because, on average, men married women two to three
years younger than them, the stock of older men was
depleted for women who waited until their thirties. This
disparity did not begin to reduce until the 1980s and 1990s,
by which time the greater number of female graduates and
professionals were depleting the number of high-status men
by taking their jobs.

If women waited longer to marry and then found it
harder to snag an appealing man, they were also increasingly
likely to divorce, or to separate from the father of a child
born out of wedlock. Although the divorce rate started its
rise in the 1950s, in the USA and the UK it was not until the

late 1960s that it began to double every decade for the next three. Whilst the rate eventually stabilised in the early 1980s, this was partly because fewer couples were marrying in the first place. That period also saw a large increase in out-of-wedlock births, rising to the one-third of all births today (although, among the middle classes, most subsequently tie the knot with the father). Women became more assertive, their confidence boosted by education, earnings and encouragement from the wider culture; on average, by 1993, in the USA, they were as assertive as men. With no-fault divorce having been introduced in the UK, the barriers to this solution were lowered by the increasingly common experience of marital disharmony (what I described as 'gender rancour' in my book *Britain on the Couch*; I put the view that men and women have never got on worse in the history of the world). In two-thirds of cases it was the wife (now more assertive) who filed for divorce, with abusive behaviour by husbands probably increasing.

It might be supposed that such dispiriting trends would have led to a reduction in the premium placed on love in relationships. In fact, the opposite was the case. In the 1960s, 40 per cent of American women said that they would consider marrying someone without loving them, so long as they had other desirable characteristics (like humour or wealth), but only 15 per cent felt that way in the 1980s. The harder it became to find committed love, the more highly prized it became. In recent decades the sums spent by those who do tie the knot have inflated: the average sum spent on a British wedding is £16,500, and for an American one, $19,000 – a market worth $40 billion in the USA. The increasing scarcity of love and uncertainties about its authenticity, made people even more desirous of it and, when it came to weddings, they were that much more inclined to make a Big Statement, on top of the increasing tendency for conspicuous consumption in all aspects of material life.

These sad developments in relations between the sexes illustrate how much Selfish Capitalism thrives upon misery. For example, high rates of divorce and separation serve it very well. Consider the money that changes hands every time it happens. There are the legal fees, the need for the departing partner to buy or rent a new home (if they buy: estate agents' fees, chartered surveyors' and solicitors' fees, mortgage) and to purchase a second set of 'essential' electrical goods (TV, DVD, stereo), furniture and so on. Finally, there is the increased consumption resulting from the increased likelihood of mental and physical distresses caused by the divorce, from compensatory overeating to alcoholism to shopaholia. In this view, Selfish Capitalism could be naturally selecting divorce and separation as a way of increasing consumption.

It is also worth reflecting on the form that American feminism took during this time. Despite having been around for a century, it now encouraged women to aspire to be 'men in skirts', as it is sometimes disparagingly described: never mind the original ideals of feminism, which were as much about men becoming like women as vice versa, the American model was of a woman who could work as long, shout as loud and compete as ruthlessly as men always have. This greatly suited Selfish Capitalism – ultimately, it has proved very helpful in enabling the rich to become still richer. In the UK in 1950, only 30 per cent of women worked, whereas today as many women work as men. If this huge swelling in the number of available employees hadn't happened after the 1970s, employers and governments alike would have found it far harder to drive the winner-takes-all, unequal bargain that is now the Selfish Capitalist norm in English-speaking nations. A substantial proportion of British mothers of small children are employed in low-paid, part-time work, in a very weak employment bargaining position. Even in highly competitive job markets (like among lawyers and bankers) women's bargaining power is decreased by the 'need' to earn large sums. That plenty of mainland West

European nations, such as France, have managed to avoid large increases in dual-income homes with small children suggests that better education and incomes for women are not themselves critical in the rise of dual-earning households. Rather, these changes have to be accompanied by Selfish Capitalism in order for women to feel compelled to work – status competition and materialism are the independent variables, not women's education and incomes. A better-educated, higher-paid female workforce is a signal achievement of the post-war period, but that should not distract us from the extent to which they have been hijacked by materialism.

Above all, from the standpoint of emotional distress, Selfish Capitalism strongly promotes materialistic values and their behavioural manifestation – compulsive consumerism. The most important single prediction of Selfish Capitalism theory is that nations which embrace it will have higher rates of emotional distress than ones which do not. There are two simple ways of testing this. The first is to examine whether rates of distress rise when societies shift from relatively Unselfish to relatively Selfish mode. The other is to compare rates between today's Unselfish and Selfish. This brings me to the most significant evidence of all.

Testing Selfish Capitalism Theory: has the prevalence of distress increased more rapidly in English-speaking nations since the 1970s, compared with 1945–1980 and compared with relatively Unselfish Capitalist mainland Western Europe and Japan?

To set it out formally, Selfish Capitalism Theory offers an explanation of differences in prevalence of emotional distress between nations. Its propositions are as follows:

1. Societies have Selfish Capitalist political economies if the success of business is judged largely by its short-term share price, at the expense of longer-term investment; if they have a strong drive to privatise collective goods, be they large ones, like utilities, or smaller ones, like school playing fields; if they provide minimal regulation of labour markets and financial services, and minimise the extent to which the taxation regimes redistribute wealth; and if they assume that consumption and market forces can meet human needs of almost every kind.

2. Compared with Unselfish Capitalist societies, ones with Selfish Capitalist governance have greater economic inequality, more job insecurity (as defined by the

International Labour Organization), poorer physical health and poorer quality personal relationships (as defined by Avner Offer in his account of the domestic household economy and the economics of 'Regard').

3. These consequences of Selfish Capitalism cause greater relative materialism than Unselfish governance.

4. A high prevalence of relative materialism increases the prevalence of emotional distress (depression, anxiety, substance abuse and low impulse control as defined in the 2004 WHO study).

5. Selfish Capitalist governance causes emotional distress.

Each of these propositions require more detailed development and testing than can be achieved here but there are two tests of the most important prediction of the theory – that Selfish Capitalist governance causes emotional distress – which can be attempted right away.

● Hypothesis 1: If a nation undergoes a shift from Unselfish to Selfish Capitalist governance, there should be an increase in prevalence of emotional distress.

- Hypthesis 2: Selfish Capitalist nations should have
  higher prevalence of emotional distress than Unselfish
  Capitalist ones.

Selfish Capitalism emerged during the 1970s in the USA and
the UK, as well as in the other English-speaking nations to
greater or lesser degrees. If its introduction accelerated the
incidence of distress in those nations, compared with relatively Unselfish, unchanged societies, that would support the
theory and be a test of hypothesis 1. The same should be
true of direct comparison of Selfish and Unselfish contemporary developed nations, testing hypothesis 2.

Testing Hypothesis 1

The most reliable evidence for examining time trends comes
from studies which have used the same methods to measure
rates in the 1950s, the late Seventies and the recent past.
Nationally representative samples of Americans were questioned about their emotional well-being by Joseph Veroff in
1957, 1976 and 1996. The same basic instruments and methods were employed in each study, making it an almost unique
project in its temporal sweep. A key question was, 'Have you
ever felt that you were going to have a nervous breakdown?',
to which 15 per cent more replied 'Yes' in 1976 than in 1957.

Between 1976 and 1996, the proportion who gave this answer was two-thirds higher still. This is a solid indication that US rates were increasing faster after 1976.

In Britain, three large, nationally representative samples born in the same weeks in 1946, 1958 and 1970 have been questioned when in their thirties or early forties. By most criteria, rates of distress almost doubled between people born in 1946 (aged thirty-six in 1982) and 1970 (aged thirty in 2000). For example, 16 per cent of thirty-six-year-old women in 1982 reported having 'trouble with nerves, feeling low, depressed or sad', whereas 29 per cent of thirty-year-olds reported this in 2000 (for men it was 8 per cent in 1982, 13 per cent in 2000). This is evidence of a substantial increase after 1982.

Another British study compared the results of a 1977 survey of 'psychiatric morbidity' in a representative sample of 5,684 people with those from a study conducted in 1985 of 6,437 people using the same methods. 'Psychiatric morbidity' included neurotic symptoms such as panic attacks and phobias as well as depression. Whereas 22 per cent of the 1977 sample reported psychiatric morbidity, this had risen to almost one-third of the population (31 per cent) by 1986. Again, Selfish Capitalism would be a plausible explanation for this increase.

A striking example is what happened in Australia just between 1997 and 2001, a period of accelerated Selfish Capitalism. In particular, consumer credit and home loans were deregulated in the mid-nineties, and average mortgages increased by 70 per cent in the ten years between 1991 and 2001. The average value of a mortgage rose from 2.8 times the average wage in 1994 to 4.2 times in 2004. Although the number of people living in a household was steadily decreasing, the size of homes increased. Between 1995 and 2004, personal debt other than mortgages nearly trebled (from A\$40 billion to A\$110 billion), and on average, personal saving has disappeared below zero. Australians each now have three times as many credit cards as West Europeans. In an explosion of materialism, much of the borrowed money is spent on imported foreign luxury goods such as cars and kitchen equipment. By no means was this all funded by the growth of the thriving Australian economy: the national debt doubled between 1996 and 2004 (up from A\$194 billion to A\$393 billion). To pay for their debt-ridden materialistic lives, Australians have had to work ever harder. Today, they work the longest hours in the developed world.

All these trends can be traced back to radical Selfish Capitalist governmental policies implemented in the early to mid-nineties, such as deregulated borrowing and employment laws. They are of special interest to Selfish Capitalism theory because it so happens that levels of emotional distress were measured in two nationally representative samples of Australians in 1997 and again in 2001. If a substantial shift towards Selfish Capitalism occurred after the mid-Nineties, was there a concomitant increase in emotional distress? Overall, the studies revealed that the proportion who were severely distressed in 2001, to the extent that they would urgently require treatment, had increased by two-thirds compared with 1997. For women it had nearly doubled, with the most dramatic increases among the under-forties. Rates had also risen substantially among those with 'only' high or moderate levels of distress.

These increases are exactly as Selfish Capitalism theory predicts and are in agreement with the international evidence that greater materialism is associated with distress. In particular, in the case of Australia two studies – the latest in 2001 – have demonstrated that materialists downplay intrinsically satisfying aspects of their lives, such as family and personal relationships, suggesting that the same mechanisms are operating as elsewhere. It is also of more than passing interest that the increases in distress between 1997 and 2001 coincided with a growth in the belief that genes cause distress – a correlation which may itself be caused by the growth of Selfish Capitalist governance at that time.

A large body of scientific studies demonstrates correlations between the conviction that psychological traits are inborn – genetic – rather than the product of nurture and society, and support for right-wing political beliefs. In general, genetic determinists are significantly more likely to be racist, sexist, homophobic and to possess Conservative political beliefs.

Other studies show that people who believe that emotional distress is caused primarily by genes are less supportive than those who don't when a relative develops distress, resulting in a worse outcome for the relative. Believers in genetics who develop emotional distress themselves are more likely to favour physical solutions (pills, ECT) and, possibly as a result, are less likely to recover. This explanation is suggested by other scientific literature showing that a considerable proportion of severe distress, including such problems as schizophrenia, is caused by childhood abuse and is a form of post-traumatic stress disorder. Treating such distress with drugs may slow the person's recovery. The muddling, befuddling side-effect of the drugs may interfere with the patient's need to understand how their delusions relate directly to having been sexually or physically abused.

For self-evident reasons, drug companies are not keen to promote any of this evidence. Although there is no conspiracy, the psychiatric establishment, most of which has close financial relationships with the drug companies, promotes the idea of 'geneticism' – that genes cause emotional distress and that drugs are the solution, acting as more or less unwitting salespeople for the pharmaceutical corporations. This is an uphill battle. Numerous international surveys suggest that the majority of people studied everywhere believe that depression and schizophrenia are caused primarily by environmental factors, such as stress, poverty and abuse.

The possibility that increased rates of both distress and geneticism are caused by Selfish Capitalism is suggested by the fact that, when two nationally representative surveys of eighteen- to seventy-four-year-old Australian attitudes were carried out, in 1995 and 2004, there was a significant rise in the belief that genes are a major cause of emotional distress. In the earlier study, 49 per cent of respondents believed that genes could be the cause of depression; by 2004 this had risen to 67 per cent. For schizophrenia there was a similar significant trend: in 1995, 59 per cent thought genes important; in 2004, that had risen to 70 per cent. The (psychiatric establishment-friendly) authors of the study speculated about the causes of the increases: 'The period between the surveys saw a lot of publicity about the Human Genome Project and the identification of various genes affecting a range of diseases. There may have been a generally increased awareness of the role of genes ...'. They may well be right about this.

Since 1995 the reading public in the English-speaking world has encountered many books and newspaper articles suggesting that evolution has shaped our species' psychology and that, on the level of individual differences, genes are crucial. However, what the above study's authors failed to examine is that there was a considerable growth of Selfish Capitalist governance in Australia during this period, based on a politico-economic creed which knits neatly together with genetic determinism. Since Australians are increasingly in the grip of these politics, they may be a great deal more open to geneticism. As more and more people, especially the young, became materialistic and distressed, they may also have been converted to geneticism as the explanation, increasing their vulnerability and decreasing the speed of recovery. As geneticists, they would have been more open to the idea of taking drugs to treat their depressions, coming to believe in a physical solution to a physical problem. This in turn would make them less able to address the childhood causes of their distress or the wider, socio-political ones, making individual or collective change for the better less likely.

The increases in distress since the 1970s in the USA, Britain and Australia do not apply only to adults. Children and young people in English-speaking nations, as well as their parents, would seem to have become more distressed. Particularly striking was a study comparing levels of distress in large, nationally representative samples of British fifteen- and sixteen-year-olds measured using the same methods and instruments in 1974, 1986 and 1999. Overall, between 1974 and 1999, the proportion of children with conduct problems doubled and with emotional ones (depression and anxiety) almost did so (up from 10 per cent to 17 per cent). Interestingly, problems in this age group are not restricted to children from low-income families. A British study surveyed large samples of fifteen-year-olds in 1987 and again in 1999, finding a large leap in distress among girls from the top social class, from 24 per cent to 38 per cent, with no increase among boys or among girls from lower social classes. More generally, several American studies have found similar changes among both schoolchildren and university students, for both sexes. Indeed, a meta-analysis of 269 different studies of American university students' and children's distress levels made since 1950 concluded that the increase in levels of distress has been so large that, by 1950s standards, the average child of 1990 is in need of professional help. That much of the increase in depression and anxiety has been in the last two decades is suggested by the British study which measured large samples in 1974, 1986 and 1999. There was virtually no rise between 1974 (10.2 per cent) and 1986 (10.5 per cent); the major rise happened between 1986 and 1999 (from 10.5 to 16.9 per cent). There has been a two- to three-fold increase in psychiatric medicines prescribed to children since the 1980s. In 1987, 0.9 per cent of all American children were already being given pills for attention hyperactivity deficit disorder but ten years later the proportion was four times greater. Similar increases have occurred in Britain. Whilst new patterns of diagnosis and the alliance of child psychiatrists with the research and marketing departments of drug companies partly explain this, there is a strong likelihood that it also reflects an accelerating incidence of real distress.

Although very far from being a watertight empirical test of hypothesis 1, the above evidence supports it, albeit that no attempt has been made to present contrary evidence here.

Testing Hypothesis 2

As a result of the WHO study of prevalence of distress in different nations, it is now clear that for developed nations there is a direct relationship between per capita income and level of distress. My analysis of these results (with Kate Pickett and Richard Wilkinson) and a separate one by Avner Offer both show that the richer the developed nation, the more distressed its people. Offer points out that once you remove strife-ridden Columbia, Lebanon and Ukraine from the equation, national per capita income explains over half of the difference in rates between countries. Other international comparisons indicate that suicide rates rise in direct relation to per capita income and economic growth. This suggests that the wholesale pursuit of materialist values at a national level, fostered by Selfish Capitalism, increases national distress.

What is more, a study I carried out with Pickett and Wilkinson found that there was a linear statistical relationship between levels of inequality in a developed nation and levels of distress (see Appendix 1). This is exactly what Selfish Capitalism theory predicts, as in another analysis I have done, with Pickett (see Appendix 2).

Unfortunately, in the WHO 2004 survey of distress in fifteen nations, only two English-speaking nations are included (USA and New Zealand). But there have been other very large, nationally representative recent studies done in the other main English-speaking nations (UK, Australia and

Canada) which can be argued to have used comparable methods. The average rate for the five English-speaking nations combined (23.1 per cent) was over twice that of the average (11.5 per cent) from the WHO study for the six mainland West European nations (France, the Netherlands, Belgium, Spain, Germany and Italy) combined with Japan. When rate of emotional distress and level of inequality are correlated in all the nations, there is again a strong, statistically significant, linear relationship: the greater the inequality, the higher the prevalence (Appendix 2). Given that Unselfish Capitalism is still relatively dominant in mainland Western Europe and Japan, this is as the theory would predict.

Similarly, if one correlates the amount of 'economic insecurity' – a marker of the extent of a nation's Selfish Capitalism – with the rates of these different groups of countries (mainland European plus Japan versus English-speaking), there is a clear relationship. Insecurity levels around the beginning of this century were measured by the International Labour Organization in ninety nations using seven different indices, including job security and certainty of income. On all the indices, workers in the English-speaking countries were found to be considerably more insecure than those in mainland West European nations or in Japan. These latter suffer half as much distress.

There are similar findings regarding differences between English-speaking and mainland Western European nations for many other factors, for example, among children. A 2007 UNICEF study of children in twenty-three developed nations found Britain's to be the worst off, unhealthier and more miserable, with the USA the next worst. Mainland Western European nations fared far better. A WHO study of thirty-three nations in 2001–2 showed that British, American and Canadian eleven-, thirteen- and fifteen-year-olds were much more liable than mainland Western Europeans to be both obese and engaged in dieting. The list of ways in which it is better to be raised in mainland Western Europe rather than an English-speaking nation is long and shaming.

The foregoing evidence supports hypothesis 2, albeit that contrary evidence is not considered here and much more rigorous tests are required.

Developing Selfish Capitalist Theory

The scientifically trained reader will rightly assert that the above tests of the theory are less than would be needed for a submission to a learned journal. Nonetheless, as a neophyte theory, these tests are at least suggestive. The work that still needs to be done can be summarised as follows (for a plucky attempt to start some of the work of teasing out causes from correlations which follows, see the New Economics Foundation report, DEFRA Project 3b: Sustainable development and well-being: relationships, challenges and policy implementations, 2005, by Nic Marks et al).

1. The definition of Selfish Capitalism needs tightening and stricter operationalisation. How does it differ from existing categories of political economy, such as neoliberalism or Free Market economics? Are each of the four defining characteristics of Selfish Capitalism correctly specified and might there not be others?

2. The relationship between each of the four defining features of Selfish Capitalism and the form and content of other features of societies governed by it needs to be tested out. For example, to what extent does the greater economic inequality of Selfish Capitalist nations – proposed as an outcome of Selfish Capitalism in the theory – result from privatisation rather than judging corporate success by short-term share price or job insecurity or the conviction that market forces can meet human needs?

3. Do studies of relative materialism support the contention that Selfish Capitalism causes greater relative materialism than Unselfish governance? Whilst there are cross-national studies of attitudes to money, similar evidence of attitudes to possessions, appearances and fame is currently not available. Tim Kasser and colleagues possess such data and will doubtless publish it for the fourteen nations where their Aspiration Index has been used. Once this is known, it can be correlated with measures of Selfish Capitalism, creating a more precise picture of which aspects of that political economy contribute most to which kinds of materialism – greater addiction to fame rather than appearances may be found in some nations, for example, with different consequences.

4. Does a high prevalence of relative materialism increase the prevalence of emotional distress (depression, anxiety, substance abuse and low impulse control as defined in the 2004 WHO study)? As we saw in chapter 1, a great many factors contribute to emotional distress. A full test of this question would need to take them into account. In developing nations where there may be elements of Selfish Capitalism (imposed by the IMF and World

Bank), there are also large swathes of population who are driven by survival materialism, rather than the relative variety. This would affect prevalence of distress, since survival materialism does not cause distress, even if the conditions which foster it (starvation, homelessness) can do so. In such countries it might be informative to measure distress amongst affluent citizens in the ruling elites suffering relative materialism, compared with poor citizens engaged in survival. It would also be interesting to distinguish between individuals who have made the shift from poverty to affluence in their lifetimes and those who are second- or third-generation affluent, either as a result of emigration or several generations of being part of the ruling elite.

5. Does Selfish Capitalist governance cause emotional distress? Whilst this may prove to be true on average, it is likely that there are a great many moderating variables. A basic distinction, as above, would be between Selfish Capitalism in developed and developing nations – relative versus survival materialism should moderate the effects of Selfish Capitalism on distress. Another significant difference would be between societies which became Selfish Capitalist without major socio-economic

upheaval, like the transition from the 1970s to the present day in the English-speaking world, and those who underwent major disruption, like most of the countries in the former Soviet Union. A fine test would be between countries from the Soviet Bloc that are wholeheartedly Selfish Capitalist and ones which are not, like Poland. Are there differences in prevalence of distress, as the theory would predict? Interesting test cases will also be the intermediate developing economies, like India and China. As outlined in *Affluenza*, China is a fascinating example. It has only partially implemented Selfish Capitalist policies. Its population would seem to be highly materialistic, but much of this is survival rather than relative. If its economic growth continues, will there be a shift from one to the other, and will this be accompanied by rising distress? At present, Shanghai has the lowest prevalence of distress in the WHO study. If the same measures are used to survey distress in ten and twenty years' time, will there be a steady increase, and to what extent will this be due to changes in category of materialism rather than other factors? This is a study that should be undertaken immediately, a perfect opportunity for testing out the fundamental causes of differences in psychiatric epidemiology.

Most important of all will be to disentangle the relations between Selfish Capitalism and a whole stew of major socio-economic processes which correlate with emotional distress. Of the many, I will pick out a few obvious contenders:

Levels of Individualism-collectivism:

In the collectivist society, identity is conferred by familial background, gender, ethnicity and class. In the individualist society, it is achieved through education and profession. On the whole, Selfish Capitalist societies are more individualistic. Does this individualism independently cause higher distress? To what extent is individualism caused by Selfish Capitalism, so that the impact of individualism on distress (if it were proven) would be a secondary effect of Selfish Capitalism?

Economic Inequality:

High inequality and Selfish Capitalism correlate; distress correlates with both. What is causing what? The theory predicts that Selfish Capitalism causes inequality which contributes to relative materialism which causes distress. But it could be that inequality causes distress without any impact on relative materialism. At least theoretically, it could even be that inequality causes Selfish Capitalism which causes materialism which causes distress.

Anomie and Alienation:

Durkheim's theory of anomie (based on the way patterns of work evolved), or Marx's theory of alienation (based on patterns of ownership of capital) would need to be tested separately from Selfish Capitalism as causes.

Moral Theories:

As has been frequently protested by the political Right, changing morality could be an independent cause of increased distress. The American political scientist Charles Murray contends that increased illegitimacy – out of wedlock births – on its own is a major cause of social breakdown, increasing crime and, by implication, distress. In the UK, Norman Dennis has reformulated this factor as the absence of fathers, Richard Sennet has pinpointed a 'corrosion of character' and Avner Offer identifies 'imprudence' and 'myopia' (short-term hedonistic economic and interpersonal behaviour). All have been influenced by the American social scientist Amitai Etzioni's claims about declining social capital, empirically demonstrated by Robert Puttnam. A decline in religious observance could also be an independent cause.

In a full account of Selfish Capitalism Theory, the relationship of all these factors would need to be examined, showing how they contribute to, or are by-products of,

Selfish Capitalist governance, and how they relate to distress prevalence.

This account of the factors needing further consideration in the development of the theory is far from comprehensive, indicating how much more there is that we need to know in order to explain international differences in distress. Nonetheless, the contentions and evidence presented here should, at the least, seem suggestive that there are significant questions in need of answers. Hopefully, Selfish Capitalism Theory, albeit a neophyte one, is a starting point for provoking further research.

In the meantime, I shall end with a chapter devoted to a more speculative aspect of the theory: the processes by which Selfish Capitalism reproduces itself.

Chapter 4
How Selfish Capitalism Reproduces Itself

As documented in chapter 3, the American political scientist David Harvey provides compelling evidence that Selfish Capitalism (or neo-liberalism) was systematically promulgated in the 1970s by an alliance of American corporations. Spending $900 million a year, they spread it around the world through politicians, academia, 'institutes' and the media. Whether or not Harvey is correct in his claims about the deliberate promulgation of neo-liberalism and its scientific bankruptcy – and, doubtless, there are many who would dispute them – there is little question that it made the rich much richer and leaves the rest of us where we were in the 1970s, in terms of income. Dual income earning has increased affluence per household but at considerable cost to the well-being of all concerned.

My theory contends that all this has also made us much more distressed but on top of that, and the subject of this final chapter, I maintain that Selfish Capitalism has a mechanism for reproducing itself which has certain parallels with Darwin's theory of evolution.

Since the 1970s psychologists and psychiatrists have increasingly favoured evolutionary theory to explain empirical and clinical findings. Not only does this lack scientific merit, it has focused attention on to hypothetical conditions millions of years ago and on the electrochemical realm of genes, distracting us away from more crucial contemporary social processes. This distraction is greatly in the interests of Selfish Capitalism, discouraging scrutiny of what may be its true purpose: to make the rich richer.

Evolutionary theory offers random genetic mutation as the mechanism by which new DNA combinations emerge and their adaptive value is held to be the principle governing whether or not they endure. Richard Dawkins specifies this principle even more precisely, namely, whether an adaptation results in the reproduction of the individual's 'selfish' genes. By analogy, whether a social form or content is selected under Selfish Capitalism depends on whether it furthers its four core elements (outlined in the last chapter: short-term share-price as the measure of business success, deregulation, privatisation and the notion that markets can meet nearly all human needs). Where Selfish Capitalism theory differs from Dawkins' is that it is falsifiable. In evolutionary psychological theory there is a grave danger of tautology. It assumes that everything about human behaviour and experience is ultimately traceable back to a hypothetical human past in which it was adaptive. This post hoc functionalism would seem to contain its conclusions in its predicates. Because something has endured, therefore, it must have served an adaptive purpose. But in that case, how could it ever be proven that something had never served such a function? As presently formulated, evolutionary psychology is incapable of providing testable explanations of the endurance of maladaptive human characteristics over millions of years.

By contrast, Selfish Capitalism theory is eminently testable, as outlined at the end of the last chapter. However, there are interesting questions regarding the purpose of Selfish Capitalism and the means by which it gained such dominance which are less empirically clearcut and take us into more speculative realms. David Harvey's contention that its purpose was to make the rich richer cannot be proven post hoc – that this was clearly its consequence does not prove it was the reason either for its original invention or its success. In this chapter, therefore, I explore further the ways in which it may have reproduced itself.

At any one time, all manner of economic, social, political and other trends are occurring in all societies. Some will enable the core defining features of Selfish Capitalism to flourish, others will inhibit or counteract them. My starting point, therefore, is to examine a variety of processes which have supported Selfish Capitalism and in this sense, could be argued to be selected by it. Most intriguing of all, I begin with theories of evolutionary psychology themselves, offering them up as an ideology which supported Selfish Capitalism.

Theories propounding genetic causes of human behaviour encourage us to regard ourselves as powerless and to rely on medicine rather than social change for salvation. Evolutionary psychology, itself, may be popular because it almost invariably provides faux-scientific justification for the Selfish rather than Unselfish Capitalist status quo. It is hard to think of a single example of a prediction made by selfish gene theory which does not accord with conservative, and especially neo-conservative, political ideology. The rich are rich and law-abiding, and the poor are poor and criminal, because of their genes, if American social scientists Richard Herrnstein and Charles Murray are to be believed: the people at the bottom of the gene pool have sunk because of their defective DNA. Men have to be real men and women have to look like 'babes' because of our ancestral past. Competitive aggression is our natural state in the lesson taken from the book of Steven Pinker. Indeed, the history of the sales of Richard Dawkins' *The Selfish Gene* may itself be an example of how ideas are selected by Selfish Capitalism.

Published in 1976, it was not until the 1980s, I believe, that it became a best-selling phenomenon. I cannot prove this because, when I sought to obtain information regarding the pattern of sales from Dawkins' publishers, they refused to release it. It is possible that their reluctance is because they know that it was only when 'no such thing as society' Thatcherism and Reaganomics took off, that sales of the book did too. *The Selfish Gene* stands on its own as an important piece of work, with literary as well as scholarly merits, which may explain why it has been more widely read than E O Wilson's *Sociobiology*, published the year before. But the *extent* of its success could be Selfish Capitalist selection. Dawkins' central contention that we exist as machines for reproducing our selfish genes was used (however unfairly) as the intellectual justification for the values of an era encapsulated by the statement 'greed is good' (as said by the character Gordon Gekko in Oliver Stone's film *Wall*

Street). Dawkins may have been cruelly (if richly) rewarded by becoming thought of as an apologist for Thatcherism and Reaganomics, just as Orwell would have been appalled at the misuses that were made of his books *Animal Farm* and *Nineteen Eighty-Four* to fight the Cold War. But Selfish Capitalist selection is a plausible explanation of the scale of Dawkins' book's success.

Indeed, this is not the first time that Darwinism has been used to justify elements of neo-liberal political economy. However uncongenial a fact it may be for the likes of Dawkins or other evolutionists, many of whom may have political views that are to the Left of centre, there is a long history linking their ideas with Selfish Capitalism and its predecessors. It was during the second half of the nineteenth century that the phrase 'the survival of the fittest' was coined – not, as is commonly assumed, by Charles Darwin, but by Herbert Spencer. Spencer argued that because almost everything about us is genetically inherited, it would be disastrous for the state to do anything to protect the weakest, for that would be as harmful as a fire service pouring petrol on flames. Not only public education should be eschewed, even public sanitation, for only then would nature take its course and eliminate the weakest, thus strengthening society. 'Partly by weeding out those of lowest development,' Spencer wrote, 'and partly by subjecting those who remain to the never ceasing discipline of experience, nature secures the growth of a race who shall both understand the conditions of existence and be able to act up to them … what can be a more extreme absurdity than that of proposing to improve social life by breaking the fundamental law of social life?' To interfere with the survival of the fittest through state welfare and health assistance could lead only to an ever-increasing lump of genetically substandard people, holding back progress.

The Englishman Spencer's theories were not popular in his homeland at the time of their publication, but in the USA he was widely read and fêted when he travelled there. His Social Darwinism became especially popular towards the end of the nineteenth century at a time when massive fortunes were being amassed. The gap between the richest and poorest today may seem large to us, but back then it was three times greater. There was fantastically conspicuous consumption at parties with cigarettes made from $100 notes, worth more than a hundred times that in today's money: the $10,000 cigarette. Amongst American rulers, Social Darwinism was explicitly used to justify the huge inequalities of wealth and the untaxed passage of fortunes to the next generation. In a speech at an extravagant dinner, the audience was told by a leading businessman that 'the law of the survival of the fittest was not made by man. We can only by interfering with it produce the survival of the unfittest.' Expanding on this theme at a Sunday-school class, John D Rockefeller declaimed, 'The growth of a large business is merely the survival of the fittest ... this is not an evil tendency in business. It is merely the working-out of a law of nature and a law of God.'

Spencer's ideas declined in popularity and after the Second World War they were replaced by the drive towards meritocracy, equality of opportunity for the poor and women, and democracy. But this rationalisation of increasing the wealth of the rich did not disappear forever. It re-emerged with a few elaborations in the form of the works of Leo Strauss and Milton Friedman. Their ideas provided the economic foundations of Thatcherism and Reaganomics, and however unpalatable it may be to Richard Dawkins, his book more than any other provided the moral and cultural underpinning, creating a favourable climate of acceptance.

Indeed, a case can be made for the view that the wide appeal of evolutionary psychological ideas is a form of American Selfish Capitalist imperialism, easing acceptance thereof. Other recent examples, usually served with lavish helpings of evolutionary psychological theorising to provide a 'deeper' justification, are the rise of Positive Psychology and Cognitive Behavioural Therapy, both of which suit Selfish Capitalism very well, both of which are largely American exports.

The American psychologist Shelley Taylor has claimed that emotional well-being is actually better if one lives in an optimistic bubble of positive illusions, deceptively rose-tinted. Americans who think that their friends like them more than they really do, who believe that bad things are less likely to happen to them than is statistically the case, or who have an exaggerated notion of their abilities, are consistently found to be less prone to depression. The depressed, according to these researchers, suffer from 'depressive realism' (a curious formulation: those who distort reality by painting it pink are healthier than those who perceive it accurately). Some American researchers have gone so far as to propose that positive illusions are a universal foundation of emotional well-being, grounded in evolution. This turns out to be an attempt to use evolutionary theory to transpose a specifically American pattern on to humanity as a whole.

In the first place, a major shortcoming of this research is that it does not take into account the fact that around 15 per cent of English-speakers have 'repressor' personalities – will say they are happy almost whatever their true state. In one study, repressors accounted wholly for the bubble of positive illusions: all the rose-tinted, bubbly ones were distressed but didn't know it (physical measures of stress, like hand-sweating, show that repressors are much more anxious than they realise); measured separately, the illusions were absent in the 85 per cent of us who were non-repressors.

On top of this, it is important to remember that artificial boosting of self-esteem is a huge industry in America, with school programmes to increase it and government task forces targeting it. Thousands of pop psychology books and scientific papers are devoted to the subject. Partly as a consequence, when Americans are asked about their self-esteem, the great majority will score theirs as high rather than moderate because their culture encourages this kind of self-appraisal. This should lead any half-sceptical person to regard the results of surveys of happiness with grave suspicion – I would go as far as to say they are worthless as measures of people's true inner states. When asked to rate their 'interpersonal sensitivity', half of Americans saw themselves as in the top 10 per cent, nationally. By definition, of course, that cannot be so. As described in chapter 3 of *Affluenza*, it turns out that the supposed universality of the bubble of positive illusions is exploded by patterns of thinking in Far Eastern nations. Far from seeing things this way, by American standards, the average Chinese person sees the world through a bubble of negativity.

This attempt to misrepresent our natural state as optimistic is attractive for Selfish Capitalism because it encourages us to be the happy clappy, consumerism-obsessed, unquestioning dupes of corporations and politicians. It has allowed the growth of a whole industry (books, therapies, management consultancy, sports psychologists) propounding positive psychology, pathologising all of the negativity which might lead people to question either their upbringing or their society. A prime example is the quick fix solution to negativity known as Cognitive Behavioural Therapy (CBT). This has recently been bought into by the British government which is intending to train 3,000 therapists to provide a nationwide network.

CBT is mental hygiene. However filthy the kitchen linoleum of your mind, CBT soon covers it with a thin veneer of positive cleaning fluids. Unfortunately, shiny surfaces tend not to last. It takes only six to sixteen sessions to scrub away mental dirt which took decades to accrue. Making the assumption that unpleasant emotions result from inaccurate thinking, CBT deliberately ignores those unsightly, difficult-to-remove marks made by childhood maltreatment, actively discouraging their consideration by the patient. Being cheap, quick and simplistic, CBT appeals to quick-fix politicians.

The economist Richard Layard has made the case for national application of this treatment on economic grounds. He claims that CBT 'can lift at least a half of those affected out of their depression or their chronic fear'. Forty per cent of people who claim disability allowance do so as a result of mental illness. Since a course of CBT costs only £750 – about the same as a month's disability allowance – the treatment would pay for itself by getting patients back to work. The £600 million cost of the new CBT nationwide service would soon be similarly recouped.

If only life were so simple. The truth is far more complicated. Take the example of Mrs B, a thirty-two-year-old mother of three who suffered from panic attacks, agoraphobia (fear of open spaces) and claustrophobia (fear of enclosed spaces). On one occasion, she had been driving through London and panicked she would never be able to find her way home, too anxious to use the map. Eventually she ran out of petrol and the police found her parked at the side of the road, sobbing. When she got home, she felt panic-stricken by being 'trapped' inside. But if she went into the garden it seemed much too big, fearing that 'I would disappear into the hugeness of the sky'. Only when her husband was called back from work did she become calm. Her doctor sent her to a clinical psychologist for ten sessions of CBT. He got her to describe the catastrophic thoughts that came into her mind during attacks, like that she was about to have a heart attack or that the room would contract and crush her. Then he asked her to consider if these thoughts were realistic and to replace them with less disturbing ones. He also taught her to think positive.

For a few weeks after the treatment ended she felt better. But within six months the symptoms returned. Contrary to Layard's optimism, this is what usually happens after CBT. At the point when the treatment finished she would have been rated a success. But the studies very rarely follow up what happens in the longer-term. As Drew Westen (of Emory University in America) and many other researchers have shown, where patients have been examined two years later, at least half of panicky ones have relapsed or sought further help. Even immediately after the end of a course of CBT, the average patient is still having a panic attack every ten days.

The results for depression are even worse. Two-thirds of those treated for depression with CBT have relapsed or sought further help within two years. Before that, when the treatment ends, the average patient is still depressed. If given no treatment, most people with depression or anxiety drift in and out of it. After eighteen months, those given CBT have no better mental health than ones who have been untreated.

It must be acknowledged that, in the short-term, CBT does have some effect. It reduces the intensity and amount of symptoms of significant numbers of people. But even this is of questionable advantage because CBT is very focused, targetting specific thoughts and behaviours in isolation. Will, a workaholic property millionaire (described in chapter 2 of *Affluenza*), is an example of how superficial this is.

After losing a small fortune (since regained), he became depressed and did CBT. He says that 'what you think is what you feel is very true. I rigidly and fastidiously try to prevent myself sitting on negative thoughts. It's like hygiene. I try and remain active, do lots of sport, outings, things that keep me occupied'. He lives, thinks and talks at a tremendous pace. He says that all his waking hours are devoted to work and makes no distinction between friends and work colleagues. It could be argued that this is good for him, except that he is involved in a constant struggle to control his thoughts, with depression always just around the corner. If he were given tests, doubtless he would be classified as not depressed, but that is not the full story.

The CBT patient is taught a fairytale to tell themselves, a relentlessly positive one. If the therapist is skilled, the patient becomes able to ignore many of their true feelings, persuading themselves and others that they are feeling good. When tested at the end of the treatment, like a well-coached pupil taking one of the exams or tests on which our government is so keen (with teachers increasingly forced to teach to exams), they often regurgitate the positive story, literally placing ticks in the right boxes of the questionnaires used by researchers to evaluate their mental state. But a few months after the teacher-therapist is no longer coaching them, their negativity or anxiety gradually forces itself to the surface and they cease telling the positive story. Retested then, they no longer tick the right boxes: it's very possible that the initial gains measured in CBT patients are a simple parroting of what they have been taught, rather than expressing their real state.

An important clue is that the great majority of the reduction in symptoms that CBT patients achieve is by the fifth session. Indeed, in 15 per cent of cases, it is after the first one. This might be because they are learning a gloss to put on their emotions, a simple one that can be learnt easily, in just one session. Another indication comes from testing the unconscious thoughts of patients who have just finished

CBT. Asked to respond to words that are flashed subliminally on screens, they react faster to depressive ones. Studies of their dreams reveal a similar hidden cache of negativity.

That brief courses of CBT are not the best answer for the commonest emotional problems (depression and anxiety) is suggested by the case of Mrs B. I treated her once a week for two years using psychodynamic therapy and by the end she had no symptoms. Many years later, she has had no reoccurrence of the problems or any new ones. Rather than using CBT, I focused on her childhood. One of eight children, her mother had been unable to care for her very consistently or responsively during the early years. This had made her a jumpy, insecure person, especially in close relationships. It soon became apparent that her panics and phobias were triggered by feeling abandoned and rejected, dating back to early childhood. Now living far away from her original family, with a husband who worked long hours in an insecure job, and with three small children to care for, she had few close friends. This isolation had reminded her of the many times as a child when she had felt lost and uncared for by a mother who was inexpressive and herself very anxious. Indeed, some of Mrs B's panicky thoughts turned out to be exactly the same as those her mother had. On occasion, her mother had climbed into her bed seeking solace, filled with irrational fears, such as that she was about to die or that murderers were about to break in on a windy night. The adult Mrs B had the same fears. Over the two years of her treatment with me, we developed a relationship which seemed reliable to her. In depending on me and not being let down, she gradually discovered feeling safe. Recalling the lack of responsiveness of her mother during her childhood helped her to see that the present was very different from her past – she was no longer a helpless toddler. On top of that, she disentangled her fears from those of her mother, so that she no longer needed to 'protect' her mother by carrying her terrors.

She had previously used CBT but it only addressed her symptoms, athough it must be admitted that she may have been unfortunate in her CBT therapist. As in every other walk of life, there are good and bad ones. At its best, it encourages volition, the realisation that I am not just an animal, I can use my human agency to make choices. The good CBT therapists have twigged that the relationship with the patient is at least as important as anything they teach – that having a sympathetic, sensible but independent shoulder to cry on is enormously helpful in itself. At its worst, the method trumpets the power of thought to triumph over emotion. In the case of Samantha, for example, a highly intelligent woman in her thirties, 'the therapist just kept telling me to call black white'. Describing her despair at her ugliness and corpulence, the therapist tried to persuade her she was neither. This was despite the fact that she had an unusually unattractive face and was very overweight. But more experienced CBT therapists have sometimes grasped that this kind of doublethink is not very helpful. If at all possible, they will see the patient for many more sessions than the mandatory six to sixteen and even, in a few cases, begin to analyse the childhood origins of the problems. But then that is not CBT. Far more helpful, in my clinical experience, are methods which go beyond the symptoms. One is called Cognitive Analytic Therapy. Initial treatment is for sixteen sessions, of which the first four are devoted to the childhood causes. In many cases, the treatment is extended if there is more work to be done. Psychoanalytic psychotherapies can be very helpful at getting to the heart of the matter, although it is very important to find a practitioner who really grasps the importance of childhood causes. An intensive programme that definitely does is The Hoffman Process, a nine-day residential course. It is a systematic, concentrated method for tackling the origins of anxiety and depression.

Whilst I know Richard Layard to be a well-intentioned, honourable man, I am suspicious of the motives of the politicians who have been attracted by the economic advantages of his wheeze. Rather than seeking to send the depressed, wounded worker back to work with a false smile sticky-plastered to their face, I agree with a saying beloved of one of my aunts, 'We weren't put on this earth to be happy'. Happiness is a brief, chimerical state. Rather than the lead of Think Positive, we should pursue the gold of insight, maturity and authenticity (as outlined in chapter 10 of *Affluenza* and discussed in chapter 6 of my previous book, *They F*** You Up*). CBT rarely confers these on anyone and I find the idea of 250 happiness centres to promote rose-tinted bubbles of positive illusions faintly sinister, since it explicitly discourages patients from considering the child-hood origins of their problems and even worse, in collective terms, it actively rejects any analysis of how the person's society could be making them ill – no wonder it so appeals to Selfish Capitalism.

A further example of American attempts to universalise American attributes under the guise of evolutionary psych-ology is in the field of sexual attraction. Evolutionary psychologists, nearly all of them male and American, would argue that, back in the primordial swamp the most success-ful hunter-gatherers attracted the prettiest wives. In this picture, prettiness is a genetic indicator of fecundity and of good 'feminine' homemaking and mothering skills. Never mind that there is no evidence at all that a woman's looks and these skills correlate or have ever correlated; but then, fascinating though its speculations may be, evolutionary psychology's urge to universalise often makes it run the risk of being ideology, not science. The evolutionary ideologist's woman looks after the children, sweeps the cave and keeps the home fires burning to cook the sabre-toothed tiger stew for when daddy gets home from his hunter-gathering.

They also base their claims about the universal, genetic nature of gender differences on surveys of patterns of attraction around the world. One survey has shown that in the matter of sexual jealousy, whereas men worry about sexual infidelity, women are more anxious that their man will become emotionally attached to another partner. Another (of fifty-two nations) shows that men are more driven by a search for sexual variety than women. Most important of all was a thirty-seven-nation survey showing that women are attracted by dominant, wealthy, high-status, older men, whereas men everywhere seek youthful nubility and do not care about the status or wealth of women.

The trouble with these studies is that they blithely assume that genes explain these patterns without testing the social alternative. When that is investigated, the genetic foundations look rather shaky. Two re-analyses of the thirty-seven-nation study, for example, have shown that in societies where women can gain access to wealth and status through education and a career rather than marriage to a man, they are less likely to be attracted by those characteristics in a potential mate. Denmark would seem to be a prime example of this: the women do not aspire to nubility; if anything, it is the men who have to use appearance to attract women.

Most recently of all, a meta-analysis of the forty-six analyses that have surveyed this issue challenged the notion that men and women are all that different, psychologically. In the great majority of traits (78 per cent), differences between men and women are either non-existent or small. It turns out that there is no difference in how good girls and boys are at maths. Girls' self-esteem is widely believed to be lower because it nosedives on entering puberty: in fact, boys' self-esteem falls just as much. In most respects, the genders communicate in the same way: forget about men interrupting much more than women and being much less self-revealing. Only a handful of the cherished nostra of evolutionary psychology survive this analysis. It is true that women do not masturbate nearly as much and they are not up for casual sex to anything like the same degree. They physically attack others dramatically less often. But the conclusion is that,

overall, to a very large degree, when it comes to gender difference we almost do start as blank slates.

The evolutionists' account of gender differences in
sexual attraction are a cornerstone of American culture (a
lesson taught again and again on television and in films,
from *Sex and the City* to *Titanic*) and directly represent a
significant portion of its economy – the money spent by
women on dolling themselves up to fit the stereotypes
demanded by the media, the sums spent and long hours
worked by men to afford the consumer signals of their
alpha-male status, claimed to be naturally required for
attracting females. Yet again, there is all too neat a fit
between the interests of Selfish Capitalism and the 'findings'
of American evolutionary psychology.

Of course, 'maladaptive' (ie contra Selfish Capitalist)
cultural mutations will arise. Michael Moore can succeed in
making films and selling large numbers of books that
deplore it, and Noam Chomsky can find a publisher (eventually – for several years in the 1980s he could find none;
meanwhile, in the last decade, Steven Pinker has made a
mint out of recycling Chomsky's original contentions about
the genetic origins of language). On the international stage,
mutant nations emerge from time to time, as is currently the
case with Chavez's Venezuela and the endurance of Fidel

Castro's Cuba, despite tremendous efforts to have them suppressed. That this work of suppression is itself documented in widely read books by American journalists and investigators also suggests Selfish Capitalism has not perfected the art of suppression. Duplicity and violence have been frequently employed in promoting the globalisation of Selfish Capitalism, if these authors are to be believed.

For example, whistleblower John Perkins, in a memoir entitled *Confessions of an Economic Hit Man*, makes the startling claim that there has been a systematic attempt by a combination of government and business in the USA over the last thirty years to force foreign governments to toe the Selfish Capitalist line. Unfortunately it is impossible to verify his claims, but if true they would suggest that proponents of Selfish Capitalism have been very active in ensuring its spread, as David Harvey has claimed.

Having dabbled with a degree in Business Administration, Perkins had to find a way to avoid serving in Vietnam. Accidentally, through a girlfriend, he acquired a patron who was a senior figure in the National Security Agency (NSA), the USA's largest and least-known intelligence service. This man arranged for Perkins to be interviewed by them and although not recruited directly, in 1971 he was recruited as an economist (despite scant knowledge of the subject) by a little-known engineering company, Chas T Main, Inc (MAIN). Like its more famous brethren, Halliburton and Bechtel, MAIN planned and built infrastructures, such as electricity or water utilities, mostly in developing nations.

Soon after his arrival at MAIN, Perkins was told by an attractive older woman that she was to be his mentor, that he had been selected to become an 'economic hit man', and that he was never to inform anyone of his new role. His job, she told him, would be to justify huge international loans to developing nations for massive engineering and construction projects, which would funnel money back to MAIN and other American companies; and to bankrupt those countries by committing them to projects far beyond their means, so that they would be forever beholden to their creditors, enabling those creditors to call in 'favours' such as military bases, UN votes, and access to oil and other natural resources. Perkins claims to have been skilfully groomed by his mentor for this task. She seduced him and he believes that she used information from his NSA interview profile to play on his insecurities to make him commit himself to the work. He summarises the purpose of his job as follows: 'to create large profits for the contractors, and to make a hand- ful of wealthy and influential families in the receiving countries very happy, while assuring the long-term financial

dependence and therefore the political loyalty of governments around the world'. That this plan would not serve the
interests of the peoples of these countries was openly
acknowledged by his mentor; making the rich richer and the
poor poorer was explicitly accepted as an intended outcome.

For twenty years Perkins plied his trade in various
Central American countries, and in Indonesia and the
Middle East. There were several levels of coercion for dealing with a non-compliant leader of a client country. The first
was the threat of bankruptcy, the second to foment civil war,
the next to assassinate the offending individual. If all else
failed, the country would be invaded.

It is difficult or impossible to test the truth of many of
Perkins' assertions. For example, he implies that Jaime
Roldós Aguilera, a socialist leader in 1980s Ecuador who
died in a plane crash, was assassinated for non-compliance,
but there is no hard evidence either way – although in
theory, if NSA or CIA agents did cause the crash, one of
them could provide incontrovertible evidence that confirms
it. Such an eventuality is not inconceivable. As it happens, I
was in Ecuador for three months doing a study of mothers
and babies shortly before Roldós Aguilera's election and
death, and had read *Inside the Company: CIA Diary* by
Philip Agee, an account of that agency's shenanigans in

Southern America in the Sixties and Seventies. Given the number of other books by ex-agents since then suggesting such things did and do go on, it is at least possible that Roldós Aguilera was bumped off. From my brief acquaintance with the Ecuador of that time, it was obvious that neither the US Government nor the oil companies would be very pleased by his plans, any more than their successors can be enthralled by the socialist goals of Hugo Chávez in Venezuela today. Were Chávez to die in a plane crash tomorrow, you would not have to be a raving conspiracy theorist to wonder whether there was more to it than pilot error or mechanical malfunction.

Perkins' claims read suspiciously like a film script, but when taken in the context of how much has been published on the subject, some of it by reputable, Pulitzer prize-winning authors, it seems likely that, over the last thirty years, US business and government have had an increasingly visible hand in promoting Selfish Capitalism and in suppressing its opposite. It is a matter of public record, for example, that the infrastructural US companies that Perkins lists in his book have close links to the current government. Vice-President Dick Cheney was Halliburton's chairman before taking up his present job, and it is also a matter of public record that Halliburton, Bechtel and other American companies have received preferential treatment in bidding for the contracts to rebuild Iraq and have been beneficiaries of many billions of dollars of US taxpayers' money. David Harvey provides persuasive evidence that since the 1970s, the IMF and the World Bank have imposed Selfish Capitalist policies on developing nations. As a condition of loans, the countries have been forced to privatise their utilities and to open their markets to foreign capital. This enables American financial interests to take over whole industries and for infrastructural companies to receive huge amounts of the money that the countries borrow.

It is rare that the USA has to actually invade the developing nation in order to impose Selfish Capitalism but Harvey points to the startling example of Iraq. Following the 'liberation' of that country from Saddam Hussein, Paul Bremer, the head of the Coalition Provisional Authority, imposed four orders for organisation of the new economy: 'the full privatisation of public enterprises, full ownership of rights by foreign firms of Iraqi businesses, full repatriation of foreign profits, the opening of Iraq's banks to foreign control, national treatment for foreign companies and ... the elimination of nearly all trade barriers'. Only oil was exempted from these arrangements, it would seem because the US government directly appropriated all revenues from

this source to pay for the war. Whilst this wholesale deregulation of business went on, the opposite was the case for
workers in the labour market – heavy regulation, so that the
right to unionise was tightly circumscribed, strikes were
forbidden in many sectors and a flat tax was imposed,
strongly weighted in favour of the rich.

Indeed, the synergy between Selfish Capitalism and the
Iraq adventure is so obvious as to hardly need explaining: as
many have pointed out, is it really likely that the invasion
would have occurred had Iraq not possessed the second
largest quantity of oil in the Middle East? What is less often
noticed is the extent to which the fabled 'war on terror' has
been a deliberate misrepresentation of the true situation. Just
as utterly bogus ideas had to be propounded in the early days
of Selfish Capitalism, like the 'trickle-down effect', so with
the justification for the war and subsequent occupation.

Just as it turned out there were no Weapons of Mass
Destruction, the sole original *causus belli*, so it now appears
that there is no war on terror. This was recently driven home
to me when in conversation with a senior figure from the
British armed forces who has close contacts with the intelligence service. I know this man to be an urbane, utterly
sensible, wholly reliable person, not at all the kind given to
conspiracy theories, either of the 'reds under beds' or of the

'high-level governmental shenanigans' varieties so beloved of the political Right and Left. He said that he knew no one in the British Ministry of Defence who accepts the notion that we are 'at war' with terror. Whilst there are disparate Islamic fundamentalist groups around the world, the misuse of the word war to denote our military relationship with these groups is wholly rejected by the British defence establishment. Unprompted, to my astonishment he said, 'I don't think the Americans actually did the 9/11 attack on the World Trade Center, and as far as I know, it was allowed to go ahead.' Pressed further, it was abundantly clear that what he meant was 'who knows? It is perfectly possible that 9/11 was something the Americans wanted to happen, but it is impossible to be sure whether they actively encouraged it or knew it was going to happen and deliberately did not prevent it'. If someone in his position believes this is possible, it goes to show the extent to which it is widely known in defence circles that the Americans were spoiling for an excuse for military action.

I asked him to explain something that has always puzzled me about the supposed threat from Islamic militants. It is now six years since 9/11 and four since we invaded Iraq, making Britain a prime target. Every so often, the police or intelligence services announce that there are

hundreds of terror cells planning mass murder in this country. But if this is really true, how on earth can we have got
away with not a single death, apart from the unfortunate
fifty-two who died in London in the attack mounted in July
2005 ('7/7')? For example, I said to him, anyone with half a
brain could kill several hundred people within a matter of
hours of deciding to do so. With hardly any imagination or
aptitude, I could hijack a large lorry, drive it to a railway
crossing, turn on to the railway line and head towards an
oncoming train. If you add in that I am prepared to die in
this attempt and that I have fellow-travellers similarly
inclined who could do the same simultaneously at other
sites, how difficult would it be to do this, or any of dozens
of equally simple ways of killing large numbers of people?
He admitted it was strange that, given the many years that
have passed since 9/11, nothing like this has happened.
America has highly porous borders, is an enormous land
mass and a disparate society with innumerable extremely
vulnerable infrastructural targets (railways, pipelines,
airports) that could never be defended. Yet not one single
American citizen has been killed by Islamic terrorists since
9/11. Are we really to believe this is because the security
services are so efficient there that they have anticipated all
the threats?

It is possible that the supposedly dangerous cells identified are populated by incompetent fantasists. It is possible
that they are fixated on relatively complicated methods, like
bombs with timers. Perhaps one or other of these is true, but
it seems equally likely that there simply are not any, or hardly
any, terrorists intent on mass murder. What very few attempts
there have been in this country – the sequel to the London
July bombings (21/7, following 7/7), the pathetically incompetent attempt to bomb a Piccadilly nightclub, the feeble
attack on Glasgow airport – have all failed allegedly due to
inefficient preparation of bombs. My informant could not say
whether these attacks had been mounted by fantasists with
little practical skill, or whether they had been sabotaged by
inside British agents who had then allowed the attacks to go
ahead, or even, mounted by terrorists who had actually been
encouraged by British agents. His point was, although hardly
anyone has died (fifty-two deaths are fifty-two too many, but
contrast that with the twenty-four Britons who die *every day*
from cancer who would not have died had they been recipi-
ents of European health care – because health spending has
been so much greater in Unselfish Capitalist Europe, cancers
are picked up earlier and more effectively treated), despite all
the furore, the occasional aborted incident of this kind
certainly justifies the huge increase in intelligence and military

budgets during a period since the end of the Cold War when such justification was becoming increasingly hard to make. Indeed, he went further. He agreed that what used to be called the Military Industrial Complex of arms manufacturers and defence forces has had considerable trouble explaining its necessity since the end of the Soviet Union. Why is it that we still need to spend £32 billion a year on the Ministry of Defence? Why is it that, in a privatisation-hungry political time, 1 per cent of the British landmass is still owned by the Ministry of Defence, much of it prime land? Consult a map of Wiltshire if you do not believe me. There is a socking great section in its centre which has no roads or urban centres marked because it is not open to the public. Is it really necessary for this prime land to be still owned by a state which is in such a hurry to privatise playing fields? At the least, could they not use the tens of thousands of hectares they occupy in less populated parts of Britain?

The War on Terror is certainly a godsend if your job is to make the case for continued defence spending. It has also been excellent news for politicians. Studies using the psychological theory known as Terror Management Theory (TMT) provide solid scientific evidence that, whether deliberately or not, politicians have been able to get elected by manipulating collective fear of attack. TMT posits that human awareness of mortality makes it our core terror; we use culture in general, and leaders in particular, to create a protective shield against fears arising from the inevitability of this demise. Four experiments were conducted before the 2004 American presidential election, designed to test TMT.

In the first, reminders of death were provided to a sample of subjects by asking them to respond to two questions: 'Please briefly describe the emotions that the thought of your own death arouses in you' and 'Jot down, as specifically as you can, what you think will happen to you as you physically die and once you are physically dead'. A control sample were given questions about watching TV. Both samples were then asked to read a highly favourable opinion of the measures taken by Bush after 9/11 and how much they endorsed his actions. Those previously reminded of their death were significantly more likely to endorse Bush's policies.

The second experiment established that, on its own, being reminded of 9/11 increased subjects' awareness of their own mortality, more so, for example, than being asked to think about an exam. The third showed that reminders of 9/11 and reminders of mortality, *per se*, were equally effective in generating support for Bush. It also proved that, whether Left Wing or Conservative, subjects' approval for Bush rose after exposure to either reminder.

The experimental coup de grace directly assessed how likely subjects were to vote for Bush or Kerry (the Democratic candidate) following exposure to reminders of mortality or 9/11. Both reminders increased Bush's vote.

Another study presented subjects with an hypothetical charismatic leader who promised citizens a significant role in a noble mission. If they had previously been reminded of their death they were more likely to want to support him. Indeed, President Roosevelt's approval ratings surged following Pearl Harbor, likewise John F Kennedy's in the Cuban Missile Crisis and George Bush senior's after the start of the first Gulf War. Blair got a similar boost once the invasion of Iraq was under way. According to TMT, a leader who has the *a priori* status conferred by being president, who has a charismatic style and who advocates strong home security with aggressive military solutions overseas, will ring the bell of our need for security from death. Mark Landau, author of the Bush study, concluded that this irrational symbolic protection causes people to vote with their hearts rather than their heads.

It is not known if Bush or Blair, or their advisers, have even heard of TMT, nor are they exactly the first leaders to have used external threats as a means of obtaining electoral support. My hypothesis is that Selfish Capitalism has proved adept at finding methods for misrepresenting its true purpose in order to manufacture popular consent. If David Harvey is correct, sometimes it has done so very deliberately, as with its $900 million war chest to provide academic, media and political support in the 1970s, and as with the conscious use of the IMF and World Bank to corral developing nations into adopting neo-liberal policies. But there is also an 'invisible hand' entailed, in which ideas and practices which will benefit the rich are automatically adopted and implemented. Since such ideas appeal to the ruling elites, they will adapt and apply them without necessarily giving much thought to the true function served, that of making the rich richer.

By the same token, perhaps Selfish Capitalism automatically, as well as deliberately, will seek to destroy anything which threatens that outcome. The list of such social mutations which are killed off by Selfish Capitalism is familiar. It abhors communism only slightly more than socialism, for those ideologies explicitly reject quick and large profits for the few. It will go to considerable lengths to destroy trade unions and plans to nationalise public amenities. It actively fights forms of capitalism which prioritise long-term investment of profit for the public good. Whilst it frequently uses appeals to chauvinism and racism to drum up popular support, in practice it discourages nationalism that creates barriers to corporate globalisation. It rejects out of hand (sometimes using specious evidence from faux-scientists) ecological evidence that it is destroying the planet. Through the control it exerts over the media, it does its best to exclude voices which challenge its predicates and discourage journalistic investigation of its activities, whether in business or on the battlefield. This media gives disproportionate space and airtime to the writings and utterances of employees of the institutes set up specifically to promote Selfish Capitalist mantra. All too many journalists, as well as nouveau riche Labour politicians, who once opposed it have seen the error of their ways (the Nick Cohens and Christopher Hitchens). Since it can be a thankless and poorly remunerated task, it is easy to see why such people have become turncoats. Although pretending otherwise, it heartily loathes family life, hastening its decline, because family life poses an authentic alternative to workaholia and Marketing inauthenticity. It far prefers nurseries to care for babies and toddlers, so that parents can swell the labour force (making it easy for employers to keep wages low), and if that results in insecure and miserable children who grow into needy adult consumers who use materialism to fill the void, all the better for profits. It strongly militates against anything likely to promote intrinsic values, such as a commitment to community, altruism, concern with beauty or authentic motives for aspirations. Whilst it may pay lip service to these, for example by espousing the value of voluntary, charitable work (because that's a way of getting tax-free welfare services), it always operates to minimise their potential threat. As I descried in chapter 12 of *Affluenza*, it hijacks our potential for authenticity, vivacity and playfulness, and instead finds ways to make money out of sincerity, hyperactivity and game-playing. Above all, from the standpoint of emotional distress, it is constantly on the alert to prevent social forms which may lead to emotional well-being. It is against any kinds of therapy or social inter-vention which will encourage intrinsic motivation, favouring only temporary expedients for emotional distress, such as pills (from which real money can be made) and, as detailed above, Think Positive cognitive treatments, which are cheap and soon return the damaged worker to their workplace, briefly conned into a false optimism. For, as advertising executives so openly admit, true contentment with what we have got is the greatest single threat to the consumerism that is indispensable for Selfish Capitalism.

Limitations and future development of Selfish Capitalist theory

Whatever the merits of these observations, the critical or scientifically minded reader will realise that they leave considerable aspects of society which are not attributable to Selfish Capitalism. This makes it all the more testable and open to further investigation. Consider some simple examples, such as the case of the decrease in the age at which we first have sex.

Throughout the developed world, since 1950 the age at which people first have sex has been falling and the number of sexual partners rising. The age of onset of puberty among girls has dropped sharply, and early pubescence leads to earlier sex and more partners. This is partly because of better nutrition and the contraceptive pill, but it is also strongly stimulated by rising marital discord: on average, a girl whose father left the family home, through divorce or separation, before she was ten will enter puberty six months earlier than one whose parents remained together; and even in intact homes, disharmony accelerates the onset of puberty. Since age of entering puberty is the strongest predictor of age of starting sexual activity, divorce would seem to be an important factor.

Selfish Capitalism theory can find numerous respects in

which these trends advantage it. The British market for children's consumer goods is now worth £30 billion. The commercialisation of childhood is a well-established fact, with well-established emotionally damaging consequences. A recent study by the American Psychological Association provided compelling evidence that advertisers sexualise girls as young as age five, making them overly concerned about their weight. Only this week, a Cambridge University review of British primary school children painted a picture of stressed and consumption-obsessed pupils.

Primed by an early childhood riddled with commercialisation, teenage romance is the foundation of a lucrative market, from the presents young lovers give each other, to the cost of the meals and cinema tickets for dating, to the expenditure at ever-younger ages, especially by girls, on their appearance (clothes, make-up, even plastic surgery in the most affluent groups). It is also worth reiterating that Selfish Capitalism is delighted to find women aspiring to impossible ideals of nubility and feminine desirability because there are vast profits to be made from these efforts (fashion, 'rejuvenating' cosmetics, hairdressing), just as it revels in the unhappiness women feel about their bodies – think profits from cosmetic surgery, diets, expensive food substitutes. Equally, traditional gender stereotypes of what is attractive in men are nurtured by Selfish Capitalism (as discussed above) because it makes them slave harder for the power, money and status that are desired by women in this system, locking the men into working longer and more competitively, just to seem attractive.

However, as with every social trend, the explanation is multi-faceted. There is considerable variation between nations in the point in time and rate of increase, in all these trends. In the case of earlier sex and more numerous sexual partners, the British were slower to adopt this pattern than the Americans, who, in turn, were slower than North Europeans. Since the latter have relatively Unselfish Capitalist political economies, there is clearly more to this trend than Selfish Capitalism. The same is true of nursery care for infants and toddlers, mentioned above; whilst it has become extremely popular (and profitable) in the USA and swells that workforce, it must be acknowledged that it has been a building block of – Unselfish Capitalist – Scandinavian nations for several decades.

Another example of a trend that cannot be cosily fitted into my model is the increase in crime since 1950. Selfish Capitalism certainly benefits from the massive costs of the crime wave. Overall, the insurance industry gains more from policyholder payments than it loses from theft. But there is the expense of sustaining a large police force, of the judicial system processing criminals once they are apprehended, of imprisoning them and of supervising them once they are released (the probation service). There is the cost to business of fraud and pilfering. It would be a complex and contentious claim that Selfish Capitalism benefited from these activities – although the trend towards privatisation of prison and rehabilitative services would be a starting point. For Selfish Capitalist benefits to be shown to be a key factor, account would have to be taken of the considerable differences in crime rates between nations and within nations over time. Indeed, the crime of violence is particularly hard to present as a benefit, yet, as I showed in a monograph published in 1995, there are good reasons to suppose that high rates are associated with Selfish Capitalism. This raises the possibility that, just as with biological natural selection, many maladaptive social developments endure despite, rather than because of, Selfish Capitalism, and that it accidentally causes a great many consequences which are adverse to it – as indeed may be true of animal evolution, although no consideration seems to be given to the idea that there may be many accidental maladaptive developments which endure. A theory will be needed to explain this, but developing and testing it is beyond the scope of the present book.

The speculations in this chapter will have been greeted with howls of fury by some readers; others may have found them congenial. My point in making them is to throw up some hares which other researchers may wish to chase and to bring into question the conventional wisdom of our time. If nothing else, I hope that it will have encouraged devotees of geneticism and evolutionary psychology to consider the purposes to which their creed has been put and to ask themselves why it became so appealing at this point in history.

Conclusion

By no means do I imagine that this book is the last word in explaining differences in distress between nations but, at the very least, I would hope it encourages others to start developing some theories – hardly any other books or scientific papers exist on the subject at the moment.

My principal conclusion is that distress is best conceived as principally environmental in origin, that it is caused by early childhood care, membership of groups within societies (class, gender, ethnicity) and, ultimately, by differences in national culture, economics, politics, social structure and, of course, of values – relative materialism being critical in the case of English-speaking nations.

In particular, Selfish Capitalism is presented as having been a major cause of increased distress in the English-speaking world since the 1970s. The consequence of this form of political governance has been very different from those claimed by its progenitors. Far from having been for the good of all, it has simply made the rich richer. Whether that was always its true purpose, as David Harvey maintains, is debatable, but there is little basis for doubting that it was the consequence.

The solution is simple. Instead of continuing with Selfish Capitalism, our politicians must start the work of persuading us to adopt the Unselfish variety. If they do so with the ingenuity, ruthlessness and audacity that Margaret Thatcher and Ronald Reagan employed in preaching their creeds, are there any reasons why they could not succeed?

The starting point is the recognition that the foundation of emotional well-being is nurture received during the first six years of life, the earlier the care, the more vital. From at least the third trimester of pregnancy onwards, there is powerful evidence that the environment, including the foetal one, profoundly affects well-being in later childhood and adulthood. A society which was putting well-being before the wealth of a tiny minority would actively encourage parents to care for their children during these early years, and provide maximum practical and emotional support to them. After the age of six, it would go to great lengths to ensure that one or other parent can be present to collect the child from school or be at home to welcome and supervise it. The single greatest damage that has been done in the last thirty years has been the pressure for both parents to work during the early years. What is urgently needed is for both men and women to reconsider the priority they put upon earning. Since men are every bit as likely as women to be capable of caring for small children, men must be under as much pressure to consider cutting their working hours. At present, it is the woman who is made to worry about the details of how a small child will be looked after if she returns to work. The man should be equally exercised.

When pressed on the Radio 4 *Today* programme (January 2007) for a single solution, I picked the idea of paying every family with a child of under three years the average national wage (see www.fulltimemothers.org for discussion of various proposals to make it easier for parents to care for their small children). One parent might choose to do it full-time, or the care might be shared between them. Above all, this would remove the necessity for dual-income earning when children are small, although it would also go a long way to raising the status of the role of full-time parent. Neither political party seems to have taken the suggestion seriously – 'vital' fiscal commitments, like the upgrading of our Trident nuclear missiles, have priority.

The present government seems far more set on separating parents from babies, so that they can be cared for badly by poorly paid strangers, rather than on keeping them together. But I do not believe we should despair. Not only do I suspect that the electorate is heartily sick of thirty years of Selfish Capitalism, there are massive global forces which will make fundamental change inevitable in the next few decades – climate warming; unsustainable American indebtedness to unsustainable Chinese economic growth; finite, declining oil reserves, to name but three.

Sooner or later a politician or party will emerge who offers a radical alternative to the hollow materialism of the present lot. They will remind us that winning or being rich are as nothing to enjoying the activity and having enough to meet basic needs. It is impossible to have a nation of chiefs without any Indians, we cannot all be famous, we cannot all be super-rich.

A mother recently told me about her eight-year-old daughter's school disco. An all-girl teenage band played, called something like the Funky Chicks, complete with slim figures, crop-tops and mini-skirts. Asked afterwards what had been most enjoyable, the daughter replied it had been getting on to the stage with the band. The mother disliked her daughter's identification with such overtly sexy models, but we agreed there was a bigger problem: in the end, there is just not enough room on the stage for everyone, not enough time for all of us to have our fifteen minutes of fame. Even if there were, it would not make us emotionally fulfilled.

One of the greatest errors made by evolutionary psychologists and conventional psychologists is to assume that our species has much to learn from other ones. Human beings are distinctly cranky, irrational and perverse. Possession of language enables self-consciousness and power over our environment, neither of which are much present in the most advanced of adjacent species. We also have a tremendous adaptability and that is grounds for optimism, as well as its opposite. Given that the English-speaking world has been hijacked by something as toxic as Selfish Capitalism for the last thirty years, it is always possible that a far better alternative is just around the corner – that, bonkers though we often seem, sanity will prevail.

Appendix 1

Emotional Distress and Inequality in the WHO Study

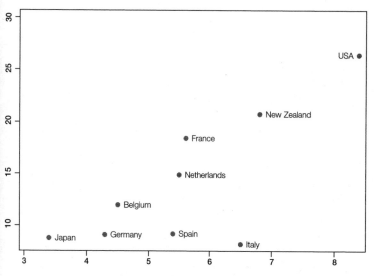

Twelve-month prevalence of emotional distress (depression, anxiety, substance abuse, impulsivity) and inequality in developed nations.

Sources
Emotional distress prevalences: for New Zealand, Oakley-Browne et al. (2006); for all other nations, Demyttenaere et al. (2004). Income inequality ratios are from UNDP (2003).

Appendix 2

Emotional Distress and Inequality: Selfish vs Unselfish Capitalist Nations

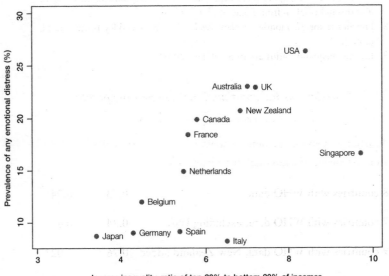

Inequality of income and prevalence of emotional distress in English-speaking nations, Western Europe and Japan.

Notes

1. The mean prevalences of emotional distress for the six English-speaking nations combined is 21.6%. The mean for the other nations, mainland Western Europe plus Japan, is 11.5%.
2. There is a strong and statistically significant linear Pearson correlation between the prevalence of any emotional distress and income inequality (see the table on the next page).
3. Prevalences in the USA, France, the Netherlands, Belgium, Japan, Germany, Spain and Italy are for 12 months and are taken from Demyttenaere et al. (2004).
4. Prevalence in the UK is for 12 months, and taken from ONS (2000, p. 32).
5. Four-week prevalence of emotional distress in Australia is from ABS (2003, p. 4).
6. Prevalence for 12 months in Canada is from ICPE (2000).
7. Prevalence for Singapore (only depression and anxiety measured) is for 12 months and is taken from Fones et al. (1998).
8. Prevalence for 12 months in New Zealand is from Oakley-Browne et al. (2006).
9. Income inequality ratios are from UNDP (2003).

Correlations for emotional distress and inequality in different developed nations

Association between income inequality and prevalence of emotional distress	Correlation	P-value
8 countries with WHO data	0.73	0.04*
7 countries with WHO data, excluding USA	0.24	0.6
9 countries with WHO data, New Zealand added	0.76	0.02*
8 countries with WHO data, NZ in, USA out	0.52	0.19
12 countries (WHO + UK, Canada, Singapore, Australia)	0.63	0.03*
11 countries as row above, excluding USA	0.63	0.09
13 countries (WHO + English-speaking + New Zealand)	0.63	0.02*

Association between income inequality and prevalence of emotional distress	Correlation	P-value
12 countries as row above, excluding USA	0.55	0.06
12 countries (excluding Singapore as a less-developed country)	0.79	0.002*
4 English-speaking countries (USA, UK, Australia, Canada)	0.996	0.003*
5 English-speaking countries (as row above, + New Zealand)	0.96	0.01*
4 English-speaking countries (as row above, excluding USA)	0.86	0.14

p-values less than 0.05 indicate a statistically significant association, indicated by *

Endnotes

CHAPTER 1

13 *The modern vogue is to seek:* see Baron-Cohen (1997).

14 *It has been argued that schizophrenia:* Horrobin (2001).

14 *Observation of monkeys suggests that depression-like:* Gilbert (1992).

15 *Arguing from the results of phenomena back to causes:* Gould et al.(1979).

17 *Even mainstream psychiatrists and psychologists:* see Plomin (1990).

18 *As described in my book:* see James (2007a); also James (2003). References for the next section, regarding genes, are also in James (2007a) unless otherwise specified as below.

22 *a New Zealand study:* see Caspi et al (2002, 2003, 2005).

23 *four studies have partially replicated:* see Eley et al.(2004); Kendler et al.(2005); Zalsman et al, in press; Wilhelm et al.(2006).

23 *in two of them:* see Eley et al.(2004); Grabe et al.(2005).

23 *Three other small studies:* see Grabe et al.(2005); Fox, in press; Kaufman et al.(2004).

23 *Furthermore, three have not:* see Gillespie et al (2005); Willis-Owen et al.(2005); Surtees et al (2006).

23 *One of these studies had a much larger sample:* see Surtees et al.(2006).

24 *Furthermore, in large studies of samples of depressed patients:* see Mendlewicz et al.(2004); Lasky-Su et al.(2005).

24 *Two of the strongest predictors:* see James (2007b).

24 *Two studies have found no greater:* see Manuck et al.(2004, 2005).

24 *Similar studies: see* Timimi (2005).

26 *Within developed nations:* eg for all these variables in European Union nations, see European Commission (2004).

26 *Someone from the lowest class:* see Fryers et al.(2005).

26 *Correlating with this:* Fryers et al.(2005).

26 *Women in most societies are about:* see Weissman et al.(1993); European Commission (2004).

26 *poor women up to nine times:* see Power et al.(1992): eg p287, see Fig 1, 2 per cent of Social Class 1 and 2 men have a 'high malaise' score versus 19 per cent of women from social classes 4 and 5.

26 *mothers with small children more so than women:* see Brown et al.(1978); Cowan et al.(1999).

26 *Men are at greater risk of alcoholism:* see Demyttenaere et al.(2004).

26 *The young suffer all the common emotional distresses:* see European Commission (2004, pp38-9); Robins et al.(1992).

27 *for example, rates of schizophrenia amongst British:* for nine times, see Thomas et al.(1993); for twelve times, Harrison et al.(1988); see also Gottesman (1992); Mckenzie et al.(1999); Read (2006).

27 *Finally, urban dwellers are about twice:* see European Commission (2004, pp48-51); Lehtinen et al.(2003).

27 *each one piles on stressors:* see Brown et al.(1978); Mirowsky (1989); Newson et al.(1976).

28 *Patterns of nurture in early life differ between classes:* see Newson et al.(1976).

28 *as well as between genders:* see Hoyenga et al.(1993).

28 *and for different generations:* see Elder (1974); De Mause (1974).

28 *Hence, being a low-income, relatively uneducated:* see James (1995); Bifulco et al.(1998).

28 *Differences in early childhood experience:* see James (2007a).

29 *risk disappears in Denmark, Finland and Norway:* Denmark, see Olsen et al.(2004); Finland and Norway, see Lehtinen (2003).

29 *the Amish in the USA:* see Egeland et al (1983).

29 *or amongst Jewish Englishwomen:* see Loewenthal (1993); Loewenthal et al.(1995).

29 *a person from a poor home who is adopted:* see Schiff et al.(1982); Capron et al.(1989).

29 *low classes are more likely to have low levels:* see Matthews et al.(2000); Manuck et al (2005).

30 *to have mutations of the gene which is thought:* see Manuck et al.(2004).

30 *only in some nations that youth in itself has become:* see Rutter et al.(1995).

30 *Regarding ethnicity, in the case of Afro–Caribbeans:* see Read et al.(2006); Mckenzie et al.(1999).

30 *there is considerable evidence that city-dwellers:* for a summary, see Read et al.(2006); in particular see Mortensen et al.(1999); Sharpley et al.(2001); Harrison et al.(2001); Allardyce et al.(2005).

30 *(200 of them in Europe since 1980):* see Fryers et al.(2004).

31 *Different instruments for measuring rates produce different results:* see European Commission (2004) eg p23, Italy has the highest rates of psychiatric disorders as measured by DSM instruments, yet the lowest rates of psychological distress.

34 *when citizens of a nation emigrate to another one:* see Kleinman (1988); Littlewood et al.(1997); Simon et al.(2002); Parker et al.(2005).

35 *the strife-afflicted area had rates of severe depression:* see Ovuga et al.(2005).

35 *A similar study done in Uganda:* see Orley et al.(1979).

35 *A more recent study of depression:* see Bobak et al.(2006).

36 *Industrialisation and urbanisation are arguably:* see Fabrega (1993); Kleinman et al.(1997).

38 *yet it is much less common in pre-industrial:* see Warner (1985); Kleinman (1988); Kleinman et al (1997); Goldner et al.(2002); Saha et al.(2005).

38 *only a quarter as common in the case:* see Kleinman (1988); note also Susser et al (1994), who found a tenfold disparity in Non-

Affective Acute Remitting Psychosis between developed and developing nations.

38   *There is also a far greater likelihood of recovery:* examined five years after initial diagnosis, 27 per cent of those in the developing world had suffered no recurrence vs 7 per cent in the developed world, and 65 per cent (developing world) vs 56 per cent (developed) had no symptoms or only mild ones at the time of re-interview. See World Health Organization (1973); Lin, KM et al.(1988).

38   *The direct causal role of urban living in schizophrenia:* see Read (2006); in particular, there is a dose-respondent effect to urbanicity, with a causal correlation between number of years lived in a city and likelihood of developing schizophrenia; see Pedersen et al.(2001).

38   *The risk of developing schizophrenia as a result of urban life:* see Mortensen et al.(1999).

38   *Some have countered that there is a tendency:* see Eaton (1980).

38   *Rather, factors of city life such as:* see Sharpley et al.(2001); Allardyce et al.(2005).

38   *A recent example compared depression in rural:* see Colla et al.(2006).

39   *Likewise, a meta-survey found:* see Paykel et al.(2005).

39   *in Britain nearly twice as much:* see Paykel et al.(2000); Allardyce (2001); Weich et al (2006).

39   *The urbanites were more stressed about housing:* see European Commission (2004, p48).

39   *an important by-product of industrialisation and a correlate of materialism:* Ger et al.(1996b).

39   *Such societies rapidly become more unequal:* see James (2000).

39   *come higher rates of emotional distress:* see Belk et al.(1985).

39   *Arthur Kleinman estimated that three-quarters:* see Kleinman et al (1997, p88).

40   *and not all experts in the field do:* eg Gottesman et al.(1992).

40   *Depending on which study you believe:* see James (1998, appendix 1).

CHAPTER 2

46 *'We have a literacy rate above 90 per cent:* see Fromm (1955, p5).

47 *Citing Marx's notion that:* see Fromm (1995, p65).

47 *'based on experiencing oneself as a commodity:* see Fromm (1995, pp20, 23).

47 *the measurement of personality characteristics in order to select:* see Paul (2004).

47 *'Skill and equipment for performing a given task:* see Fromm (1995, pp22, 23).

48 *just being bright does not predict success:* see Hogan et al.(1994); Ferris et al (2001); Board et al.(2005).

48 *by characteristics such as Machiavellianism and chameleonism:* for Machiavellianism, see Pandey et al.(1987); Fehr et al.(1992); for chameleonism, Giacolone et al.(1989); Kilduff et al.(1994); Judge et al.(1994).

48 *'What matters to the marketing character:* see Fromm (1995, p34).

48 *'A great deal of what goes under the name:* see Fromm (1995, pp34-36).

49 *'a passive, empty, anxious, isolated person:* see Fromm (1995, p69).

49 *'Boredom comes from the fact that man:* see Fromm (1995, p79).

49 *'He does indeed save time with his machines:* see Fromm (1995, pp80, 82).

50 *'The more anxious he becomes, the more he must consume:* see Fromm (1995, p71).

50 *'there is an enormous fear in many social circles:* see Fromm (1995, p71).

51 *'By their nature, [socially generated] greed and the desire:* see Fromm (1995, p38).

51 *'What the economy needs most of all:* see Fromm (1995, p70).

52 *'cannot be defined in terms of the adjustment of the individual:* see Fromm (1955, p70).

52 *'Nothing is more common than the idea:* see Fromm (1955, p3).

53 *'We live in an economic system:* see Fromm (1955, p5).

54 *'Grand generalisations about what is wrong:* see Ingleby (2002).

55 *the analysis is far from flawless (see endnote):* Ingleby points out that to a significant extent, Fromm's thinking is the liberal moralising of a humanist, dressed up as science. For example, in setting out his version of universal human nature, Fromm rejects both Freud's account of an individual whose instincts are eternally pitted against society's constraints and the more conventional psychiatric view of healthy individuals as ones whose good genes enable them to conform to the status quo (ones with bad genes are the mentally ill), with the health of society taken as given. Fromm's alternative view is a man who is set apart from the animals by possession of uniquely human mental capacities, like self-awareness, reason and morality. Whilst we have biological needs, like for food and sex, the real tension is between these and our higher mental abilities which create the potential for a volition that transcends mere genetics, rather than between individual and society. This is presented as the human situation, one that exists in all cultures and yet Fromm's great point is that different ones offer very different opportunities for self-realisation. Ingleby explains that the problem is a confusion between what Fromm feels man ought to be and what he is. Because Fromm is ultimately a humanist moraliser, he is primarily concerned with man's potential self rather than the actual humans around him in the present day. With psychologists now the priests of modern life, writes Ingleby, Fromm 'sounds as though he is preaching. The trouble with preaching is that the pulpit is placed several feet above the heads of the congregation. Many of Fromm's criticisms seem, indeed, no more than the distaste of an educated European still suffering, after more than twenty years, from culture-shock. In the end, one is left wondering what the real problem is. Is the average American alienated from himself, or is Erich Fromm simply alienated from him? … Only the culture of his own class is true culture: the rest is dismissed as an opiate … Modern man is a robot but one suspects this is because Fromm hasn't gone out to meet enough' (xlv-xlvi, Ingleby, 2002). Ingleby continues (xlvi) that

'however much one detests consumerism, one cannot plausibly claim that it is aimed at a purely passive individual' and points to the very active and angry complaints of consumers when their gratifications are not met.

56 *In 1993, the American psychologists:* see Kasser et al.(1993).

57 *a sample of eighteen-year-olds not at university:* see Kasser et al.(1993).

58 *In a series of studies it was soon discovered:* see Kasser (2002, pp9-13).

58 *This was true in Russian and German students:* see Ryan et al.(1999).

58 *A community sample of New Yorkers:* see Kasser (2002, p10).

58 *These findings were repeated for an American:* see Kasser (2002, pp11-12).

59 *three different studies went on to investigate:* see Williams et al.(2000); Kasser et al.(2001).

59 *A further series of studies involving more than 500:* see Kasser (2002, p13).

59 *A study of more than 700 twelve- to twenty-year-olds:* see Cohen et al.(1996).

60 *four different surveys found that:* see Kasser (2002, pp18-19).

60 *Other market researchers:* see Kasser (2002, pp20-21).

60 *However, the same materialism-misery correlation:* see Kasser (2002, p21).

60 *Finally, a review of studies of more than 7,000 university students:* see Diener et al (2000).

61 *A recent survey of Britons showed that fully 80 per cent:* see NOP, May, 2006, for BBC TV Happiness Formula series.

61 *In accord with a large body of evidence:* see Kasser (2002, pp23-28).

62 *Kasser asked one sample of students to write short essays:* see Kasser et al.(2000).

62 *Self-doubt, a form of insecurity:* see Ger et al.(1996a); Chang et al.(2002).

62 *Americans who were beginners at tennis:* see Braun et al.(1989).

63   *A more recent experiment established:* see Chang et al.(2002).

63   *an in-depth study of students' dreams:* see Kasser et al.(2001b).

64   *One study measured materialism in 261:* see Rindfleisch et al.(1997).

64   *materialism is higher amongst children raised in poor homes:* see Kasser (2002, pp34-35).

64   *In a study of 50,000 people:* see Inglehart et al.(1994).

65   *women were more materialistic in their preferences:* see Kasser et al (1999).

65   *The materialistic are one-and-a-half times:* see Cohen et al.(1996).

65   *Kasser found that materialists' relationships:* see Kasser et al.(2001).

65   *during the previous six months materialists:* see Sheldon et al.(2001).

66   *Kasser's in-depth study of dream:* see Kasser et al.(2001b).

66   *leads the materialists to devalue intimate relationships:* see Richins (1992); Kasser et al (1993); Cohen et al.(1996, p48); Ryan et al.(1999); Schmuck et al.(2000); Keng et al.(2000).

66   *They are less likely to endorse:* see Kasser (2002, pp64-65).

66   *One study, of forty different cultures:* see Schwartz et al.(1995).

66   *an experiment with four- to five-year-old boys:* see Goldberg et al.(1978).

67   *materialists watch more television:* for refs to studies showing this in Denmark, India, Hong Kong, Australia and USA, see Kasser (2002, p124, footnote 17).

67   *Materialists have particular traits:* see Belk (1985); McHoskey (1999); Khanna et al.(2001).

68   *Asked in one study to spend:* see Richins et al.(1992).

68   *they were less prepared to help others:* see Sheldon et al.(1995).

68   *Materialistic students in India, the USA and Denmark:* see Khanna et al.(2001).

68   *In an experiment providing opportunities:* see Sheldon et al.(2000).

68   *which has shown many times over that such people:* see Fehr et al.(1992).

69 *When a sample of 250 students were assessed:* see McHoskey (1995b); McHoskey (1999); see also, for indirect evidence linking machs with materialism via personality disorder (which correlates with materialism), Christoffersen et al.(1995); McHoskey (1995a); McHoskey (1998).

69 *materialists are also more likely to be hyper-competitive:* see Ryckman et al.(1994); Bing (1999).

69 *They are also more liable to be chameleons:* Machs and high self-monitors overlap in their concern with impression management, see Ickes (1986), so if one is materialistic, the other is likely also to be; high self-monitors also share many traits with the (materialistic) marketing character, as measured by Saunders (2000); Snyder et al.(1986); Kilduff et al.(1994).

69 *to suffer Personality Disorder:* see Cohen et al.(1996).

70 *The thousands of people who have filled:* see Kasser (2002, p75).

70 *Studies by other researchers have found the same:* see Abramson et al.(1995); Schwartz et al.(1995).

70 *materialists (in India and the USA:* see Khanna et al.(2001).

70 *Another study, of American and South Korean:* see Sheldon et al.(2001b).

71 *more likely than non-materialists to have low self-esteem:* see Sheldon et al.(1995); Chan et al (2000; Kasser et al.(2001a).

71 *Studies show that even if goals are achieved:* Baumeister (1993).

72 *prone to narcissistic or other defences:* see Kasser (2002, pp48-51); Twenge et al.(2003).

72 *Materialists who suffer a reverse:* see Emmons (1987); Rhodewalt et al.(1998).

72 *people with such unstable, shaky self-esteem:* see Kernis et al.(1993).

72 *an equally excessive hostility:* see Bushman et al.(1998); Kernis et al.(2000).

72 *when people are praised for aspects:* see Schimel et al.(2001).

73 *Materialists' low self-esteem derives from exaggerated ideas of what wealth and possessions can deliver:* see Sirgy (1998).

73 *Materialistic students asked to characterise:* for studies of viewers

in Australia ... Denmark and India, see Khanna et al.(2001); for Hong Kong, see Cheung et al.(1996); for Finland, see Murphy (2000); for Australia, see Saunders et al.(2000); for USA, see Kasser et al.(2001a).

74   *a study of elderly Americans:* see Rahtz et al.(1988a).

74   *Another study, of 1,200 adults:* see Sirgy et al.(1998).

74   *people often switch on the TV:* see Zillman (1988).

74   *a delicious way to very briefly cheer oneself up:* see Moskalento et al.(2003).

74   *people who use TV to avoid being conscious:* see Nordlund (1978).

75   *A review of seventy-nine studies:* see Fejfar et al.(2000).

75   *Sundry other studies:* see Sigman (2005, pp163-64, 187-98, 321).

75   *we lack company because we watch too much:* see Finn et al.(1988).

75   *both lower self-esteem and increase depression:* see Morgan (1984); Sigman (2005, pp163-64, 187-98, 321).

75   *this sometimes does work in the short term:* see Finn et al.(1988); Preston et al.(1994).

75   *in the longer term it serves only:* see Richins (1991); Richins (1995).

75   *students who had been shown the results of a test:* see Moskalento et al.(2003).

75   *Another experiment:* see Moskalento et al.(2003).

76   *A study of American TV content:* see Gerbner et al.(1976).

77   *In a seminal 1970s study:* see Kenrick et al.(1980).

77   *a conclusion borne out by further experiments:* see Kenrick et al.(1989).

77   *For his next trick, Kenrick:* see Kenrick et al.(1989).

77   *male American secondary school and university teachers:* see Satoshi et al.(2000).

78   *Kenrick found that when women were shown slides:* see Kenrick et al.(1993; Kenrick et al.(1994).

78   *This added to a growing body:* see Groesz et al.(2002); Gutierres et al.(1999).

78   *the effect of being unusually attractive:* see Krebs et al.(1975).

78   *Discontent of women with their bodies:* for example, Bread for Life, 1998, Pressure to be Perfect, London: Flour Advisory Bureau.

78   *A meta-analysis of twenty-five studies:* see Groesz et al.(2002).

78   *a study in Fiji:* see Becker et al.(2002).

78   *a Chinese study found that increased:* see Ma et al.(2002); for similar results in Mexico, see Hernandez et al.(1999).

79   *Silverstein began by showing:* see Silverstein et al.(1986a); Silverstein et al (1986b).

79   *Silverstein established that thinness:* see Silverstein et al.(1988).

80   *Disordered eating in modern girls:* see Blatt (1995).

80   *Girls from fee-paying schools are more at risk:* see Mann et al.(1983); Walkerdine et al.(1989).

80   *upper-class girls are more likely:* see Dornbusch et al.(1984); Wolfe et al.(1996); Lucey (1996); Levine (2006).

80   *Silverstein demonstrated that women undergraduates:* see Silverstein et al.(1988).

80   *A further study of women students:* see Silverstein et al.(1990).

80   *Silverstein's coup de grace:* see Silverstein et al.(1991).

81   *This was shown in three more recent:* see Richins (1991).

82   *it used to be thought:* see James (1998, pp103-04).

82   *When a large sample of Americans:* see Johnson et al.(2002); Zimmerman et al.(2005); Anderson et al.(2003).

83   *Hennigan took advantage:* see Hennigan et al.(1982).

85   *'Intelligence has been redistributed:* see Young (1958, p14).

85   *In the past, 'government by the people:* see Young (1958, p80).

85   *'matching of intelligence and job:* see Young (1958, p114).

86   *'What a change there has been!* see Young (1958, p152).

87   *'There was no need:* see Young (1958, p116).

87   *'For hundreds of years society:* see Young (1958, p30).

87   *In winning this battle in Young's dystopia:* see Young (1958, p36).

88   *'The greater the frustrations:* see Young (1958, p110).

88   *'Every advance towards greater equality of opportunity:* see Young (1958, p131).

88 *'improvement of communications helped*: see Young (1958, p132).

89 *The working classes were 'sharing*: see Young (1958, p140).

89 *Labour politicians 'scrapped the appeal*: see Young (1958, p140).

89 *as Young explained, 'stupid children'*: see Young (1958, p133).

89 *only to have their self-regard shattered*: see Young (1958, p107).

90 *Countless studies show that people in English-speaking*: see Taylor et al.(1994); Mezulis et al.(2004).

90 *Evidence has accumulated*: see James (1998, for facts in this paragraph, see pp112-13).

91 *There is evidence that ... they have actually fallen*: eg 'Ministers urged to step up skills drive despite record GCSE results', Alexandra Smith, Thursday August 24, 2006, www.guardianunlimited.co.uk

91 *There is also good evidence that grade inflation*: eg 'Is the gold standard looking tarnished?', John Crace and Rebecca Smithers, Tuesday August 15, 2006, www.guardianunlimited.co.uk

93 *In 1977, 31 per cent of Etonians*: The Bursar's office, Eton College, personal communication.

94 *According to Diane Ruble*: see James (1998, pp116-19) for references and greater detail regarding Ruble's work.

99 *Richard Ryan distinguishes two ways*: see Grolnick et al.(1997); Ryan et al.(2000); Assor (2004, pp49-55) for a brief review.

100 *With regard to a strong desire*: see Kasser et al.(1995).

100 *Tim Kasser followed up seventy-nine adults*: see Kasser, T et al.(2002).

101 *110 American students of both sexes*: see Assor et al.(2004).

102 *Ryan's second study provided strong evidence*: see Assor et al.(2004).

103 *in a sample of disabled children*: see Frey, KS (1987).

103 *West and Sweeting*: see West et al.(2003).

104 *An American study, of more than 250 upper*: see Luthar et al.(1999).

104 *In another study, of 302 affluent American*: see Luthar et al.(2002).

105 *One study of the gravity of American:* see Benton et al.(2003).

105 *Another study showed that self-esteem:* see Crocker et al.(2002).

105 *A study of 122 American:* see Crocker et al.(2003b).

105 *A particularly thorough study of 642 students:* see Crocker et al.(2003b).

106 *This is borne out by studies showing:* for full access to many of the papers demonstrating the contentions in this paragraph, go to the Self-Determination website and look under education, health care and work/organisational: http://www.psych.rochester.edu/SDT/publications/index.html

107 *In an American study of 460 parents:* see Ablard et al.(1997).

109 *Three studies have questioned:* Carver et al.(1998); Srivastava et al.(2001); Malka et al.(2003).

109 *In 1998, Charles Carver and Eryn Baird:* see Carver et al.(1998).

111 *This line of thinking was taken:* see Srivastava et al.(2001).

113 *The third study, published in 2003:* see Malka et al.(2003).

114 *Indeed, 128 studies have found:* see Deci et al.(1999).

115 *In a 2004 paper, subtitled:* see Sheldon et al.(2004b).

116 *Kasser's conclusion bears quoting:* see Sheldon (2004b).

CHAPTER 3

121 *The economic and theoretical roots of Selfish Capitalism:* see Galbraith (1970 pp48-55).

121 *The American political scientist David Harvey:* see Harvey (2005, p2).

122 *the Washington Consensus:* see, ILO (2004, pp19-20).

124 *a vast body of evidence:* see Henrich (2005).

124 *Most crucially, what kind of society:* see Hernich et al.(2005).

125 *although it is highly questionable whether:* see Offer (2006, p99).

126 *(although, again, it is doubtful that this is actually what is achieved):* see Froud et al.(2006); Offer (2006, p124, figure 6.4).

127 *In Britain, the top 1 per cent:* see Harvey (2005, p17).

127 *Internationally, the income gap:* see Harvey (2005, p19).

127 *The world's richest 200 people:* see Harvey (2005, p35).

127 *Real wages (adjusted for inflation):* see Harvey (2005, p25).

128 1. *By women becoming as likely:* see Offer (2006).

128 2. *Working hours have substantially:* see Offer (2006).

128 *global annual rates of economic growth:* see Harvey (2005, p154).

128 *A recent analysis of income distributions:* see Wolff (2000, Recent Trends in Wealth Ownership 1983-98), in www.levy.org/docs/wrkpap/papers/300.html; Piketty et al.(2006).

129 *in a longer historical perspective:* see Galbraith (1970, p97).

129 *since the 1970s only the top fifth:* see Offer (2006 p274).

130 *David Harvey sets the scene:* see Harvey (2005, p15).

131 *its membership grew:* see Harvey (2005, p42).

131 *spending $900 million:* see Harvey (2005, p43).

135 *private industry in the USA received (and receives):* see Hutton (2002, p153).

136 *According to the economic journalist Will Hutton:* see Hutton (2002).

137 *There was a profound change in executives' remuneration:* see Hutton (2002, chap 5); Piketty (2006).

138 *As recently as 1990, only 2 per cent:* see Hutton (2002, p32).

138 *executives increasingly demanded money:* see Dunford et al.(2005).

138 *By 2001 there were 4,000:* see Hutton (2002, p160).

138 *the USA's poor are less:* see Mishel et al.(2001, p 395).

139 *A white-skinned American:* see Hauser et al.(2000).

139 *a 1965 study showed:* see Wenglingsky (1997).

139 *students whose families were from the top one-quarter:* see Hutton (2002, p195).

139 *Definitive analysis of the causes:* see Lemann (1999).

139 *These facts caused 120 American billionaires:* this was known as the Campaign for Responsible Taxation, see Hutton (2002, p192).

139 *When President Bush Jr:* see Hutton (2002, p226).

139 *when a senior politician:* Richard Grasco, chair of the New York Stock Exchange, 1997, cited in Hutton (2002, p226).

140 *In Britain after 1978, something very similar occurred:* for evidence of assertions in this paragraph see Hutton (2002, chap 8).

140 '*The fundamental strength of the American:* see Hutton (2002, p262).

140 *the proportion of the workforce employed in financial services:* see Offer (2006, p256).

141 *In pricing the nationalised assets:* see Florio (2004).

141 *Investors in deprivatised industries achieved huge windfalls:* see Offer (2003, p27); Why has the Public Sector Grown So Large in Market Societies? The Political Economy of Prudence in the UK, c.1870-2000, www.nuff.ox.ac.uk/Economics/History/Paper44/oup44.pdf

141 *up from 19 per cent of all children:* see James (1995, p102).

142 *The Americanisation of Airstrip One:* see Hutton (2002, chap 8).

142 *Whilst there were important differences:* see Offer (2006, p364).

143 *he has said:* see Hutton (2002, p2002).

144 *The richest 0.3 per cent now own:* see James Meek, 17 April 2006, www.guardianunlimited.co.uk

146 *even this has been a mixed blessing:* see Rutter (2006).

146 *According to a recent paper:* see Kapur et al.(2006).

150 *A study of sixteen developed nations:* see Alderson et al.(2002).

150 *In a ranking of nations according:* see Nationmaster, www.nationmaster.com/graph-T/lab_reg

151 *The differences in unconditional entitlements to public services:* see Hutton (2002, chaps 7-9).

151 *Whereas 63 per cent of Britons:* see Lipset et al (2000).

151 *In Europe, on average:* see Lipset et al (2002).

151 *in a sample of 1,200 Britons in 2007:* from Zenployment study, Norwich Union, see http://www.norwichunion.com/press/stories/3240-britains-bosses-to-face-a-rush-of-resignations-as-fortysome-thing-workers-chase-fulfilment.htm

152 *there was no rise in income:* see Hutton (2002, pp38, 191, 206).

152 *Families living on a dual income:* see Offer (2006, p254, fig 11.4).

153 *The USA has spent 2 per cent:* see Offer (2006, p123, fig 6.3).

153 *After 1980, personal saving:* for facts in this paragraph see Offer (2006, pp63-68).

154 *Part of this change entailed housing costs:* for facts in this paragraph see Offer (2006, pp282-86).

154 *The physical as well as the mental:* for facts in this paragraph see Offer (2006, pp286-92).

155 *Of the many background factors:* for facts in this paragraph see Offer (2006, chap 7).

157 *increasing by 3 to 5 per cent:* see Offer (2006, p255).

158 *By the 1990s, nearly all:* see Offer (2006, p243, fig 11.1).

159 *university-educated men:* see Offer (2006, p324).

159 *the distribution of housework:* see Offer (2006, pp319-20).

160 *households of lesbians:* see Lewin (1993, pp130-34).

160 *which the man earned less than the woman:* see Brines (1994).

160 *Women, especially the well educated:* see Offer (2006, pp316-23).

160 *The high-achieving childless woman:* see Offer (2006, p330).

160 *For one thing, by the 1980s:* see Offer (2006, p243, fig 11.1).

161 *men continued to prize nubility:* see Kenrick et al.(1992).

161 *there was an actual disparity in the ratio:* see Offer (2006, p155, fig 7.4).

161 *Although the divorce rate started its rise:* see, James (1998, pp150-52).

162 *Women became more assertive:* see Twenge (2001).

162 *what I described as 'gender rancour':* see James (1998, chaps 5 and 6).

162 *In the 1960s, 40 per cent of American:* see Simpson et al.(1986).

163 *the sums spent by those who do tie the knot:* see Offer (2006, p311).

163 *The increased likelihood of mental and physical distresses:* see James (1998, p150).

164 *A substantial proportion of British mothers of small children:* see Hakim (2000, p103, table 4.4).

165 *women's education and incomes:* see Offer (2006, p243, fig 11.1).

168 *Joseph Veroff in 1957, 1976 and 1996:* see Swindle et al.(2000).

169 *In Britain, three large, nationally:* see Ferri et al.(2003, p231, table 8.8).

169 *Another British study compared the results of a 1977:* see Lewis et al.(1993).

170 *average mortgages increased by 70 per cent:* see Hamilton (2005, p20).

170 *The average value of a mortgage:* see Hamilton (2005, p71).

170 *personal debt other than mortgages:* see Hamilton (2005, p73).

170 *three times as many credit cards:* see Hamilton (2005, p102).

170 *(up from A$194 billion to A$393 billion):* see Hamilton (2005, p82).

170 *the longest hours in the developed world:* see Hamilton (2005, p86).

170 *policies implemented in the early to mid-nineties:* see Hamilton (2005, p203); Worthington (2006).

171 *Overall, the studies revealed:* see ABS Health Surveys (2003, p4).

171 *In particular, in the case of Australia:* see Sirgy et al.(1998); Ryan et al.(2001).

172 *A large body of scientific studies:* putting together the evidence from these two reviews of the evidence: see Jost et al.(2003); Keller (2005).

172 *Other studies show:* reviewed in Read et al (2004b); see also Read et al.(2006).

172 *This explanation is suggested by:* for a current review see Read et al.(2005).

173 *Although there is no conspiracy:* see Moncrieff (2006); Healy (1997).

173 *Numerous international surveys:* reviewed in Read et al.(2006).

173 *The possibility that increased rates:* see Jorm et al.(2005).

173 *authors of the study:* see Jorm et al.(2005, p766).

174 *there was a considerable growth of Selfish Capitalist:* see Hamilton (2005, p203); Worthington (2006).

175 *Children and young people in English-speaking nations:* see Rutter et al.(1995); Collishaw et al.(2004).

175 *Particularly striking was a study:* see Collishaw et al.(2004).

175 *A British study surveyed:* see West et al.(2003).

175 *a meta-analysis of 269:* Twenge (2000).

176 *In 1987, 0.9 per cent of all:* see Offer (2006, p349).

176 *Similar increases have occurred in Britain:* see Timimi (2005).

177 *My analysis of these results:* see appendix 2 and Pickett et al.(2006).

177 *a separate one by Avner Offer:* see Offer (2006, p348).

177 *Other international comparisons:* eg see Eckersley et al.(2002); Jungeilges et al (2002).

177 *a study I carried out:* see Appendix 2; Picket et al.(2006).

178 *Insecurity levels around the beginning:* see ILO (2004).

179 *A 2007 UNICEF study:* see UNICEF (2007).

179 *A WHO study of thirty-three nations:* WHO (2002).

CHAPTER 4

189 *there is a grave danger of tautology:* see Gould et al.(1979); Gould (1988, p30, pp 47-48).

189 *is incapable of providing testable:* for an impressive attempt to define the epistemology whereby human universals – as opposed to *Just So* stories about their origins – may be scientifically established, see Norenzayan et al (2005).

190 *Richard Herrnstein and Charles Murray:* eg see Murray (2000).

191 *Pinker:* see Pinker (2003).

192 *the phrase 'the survival of the fittest':* cited by Galbraith (1970, p74).

192 *'Partly by weeding out:* cited by Galbraith (1970, p74).

193 *back then it was three times greater:* see Piketty et al.(2006, p13, fig 3).

193 *There was fantastically conspicuous consumption:* cited by Galbraith (1970, p75).

193 *In a speech at an:* cited by Galbraith (1970, p76).

194 *Expanding on this theme:* cited by Galbraith (1970, p76).

195 *an optimistic bubble of positive illusions:* see Taylor et al.(1994); Dunning et al.(2004).

195 *Some American researchers have gone so far:* see Mezulis et al.(2004).

196 *In one study, repressors accounted:* see Myers et al.(2000).

196 *artificial boosting of self-esteem:* see Heine et al.(1999, p778).

196 *when Americans are asked about their self-esteem:* see Heine et al.(1999); Ryan et al.(2003).

196 *When asked to rate their 'interpersonal sensitivity':* see Myers (1987).

197 *the average Chinese:* Heine et al (1999).

198 *The economist Richard Layard:* see London School of Economics and Political Science, 'LSE Depression Report urges choice of psychological therapy for all', www.lse.ac.uk/collections/ pressAndInformationOffice/newsAndEvents/archives/2006/LSED epressionReport.htm

199 *Drew Westen:* for all the studies of CBT mentioned here, see Westen et al.(2004). This paper can be accessed on the internet: www.psychsystems.net/lab/type4.cfm?id=400&section=4&source =200&source2=1#2004; see also Westen et al (2004).

205 *Evolutionary psychologists, nearly all of them male and American:* see Buss (1989).

206 *One survey has shown that in the matter:* see Buss (2000). However, for evidence that the gender difference disappears when, instead of being asked about a hypothetical infidelity (on which Buss's research is based – 'how would you react if ...'), they are asked after an actual infidelity; see Harris (2002).

206 *Another (of fifty-two nations):* see Schmitt (2003); Schmitt (2005).

206 *Most important of all was a thirty-seven-nation:* Buss (1989).

206 *Two re-analyses of the thirty-seven-nation study:* Eagly et al.(1999); Kasser et al.(1999).

207 *Most recently of all, a meta-analysis:* see Shibley Hyde (2005).

219 *Four experiments were conducted:* see Landau et al.(2004).

220 *Another study presented subjects:* see Landau et al.(2004).

224 *the age at which people first have sex has been falling:* see Wellings et al (1994); for latest British figures go to www. esrcsocietytoday.ac.uk

224 *on average, a girl whose father:* for several references, see James (2007, p323, footnotes 119).

225 *The British market for children's consumer goods:* see Compass (2006).

225 *with well-established emotionally damaging consequences:* see Compass (2006).

225 *A recent study by the American Psychological Association:* see American Psychological Association (2007).

225 *a Cambridge University review:* see Primary Review 2007-10-12.

226 *slower than North Europeans:* for Sweden, Lewin (1982; Germany, Clement et al.(1984).

227 *as I showed in a monograph:* see James (1995).

Bibliography

Ablard, K.E. et al., 1997, 'Parents' achievement goals and perfectionism in their academically talented children', *J of Youth and Adolescence*, 26, 651–67.

Abramson, P.R. et al., 1995, *Value Change in Global Perspective*, Ann Arbor: University of Michigan Press.

ABS (Australian Bureau of Statistics), 2003, 'K10 ranges to approximate levels of psychological distress', in *Use of the Kessler Psychological Distress Scale in ABS Health Surveys*, Section 3.1, catalogue no. 4817.0.55.001, Canberra: Australian Bureau of Statistics.

Alderson, A.S. et al., 2002, 'Globalisation and the great U-turn: Income inequality trends in 16 OECD countries', *American J of Sociology*, 107, 1244–99.

Allardyce, J. et al., 2001, 'Comparison of the incidence of schizophrenia in rural Dumfries and Galloway and urban Camberwell', *British J of Psychiatry*, 179, 335–9.

Allardyce, J. et al., 2005, 'Social fragmentation, deprivation and urbanicity: Relation to first-admission rates for psychoses', *British J of Psychiatry*, 187, 401–6.

Anderson, C.A. et al., 2003, 'The influence of media violence on youth', *Psychological Science in the Public Interest*, 4(3), 81–110.

Assor, A. et al., 2004, 'The emotional costs of parents' conditional regard: A self-determination theory analysis', *J of Personality*, 72(1), 47–88.

Baron-Cohen, S., 1997, *The Maladapted Mind: Classic readings in evolutionary psychopathology*, Hove, Sussex: Psychology Press.

Baumeister, R., 1993, *Self-Esteem: The puzzle of low self-regard*, New York: Plenum Press.

Becker, A.E. et al., 2002, 'Eating behaviour and attitudes following prolonged exposure to television among ethnic Fijian adolescent girls', *British J of Psychiatry*, 180, 509–14.

Belk, R.W. et al., 1985, 'Materialism: Trait aspects of living in the material world', *J of Consumer Research*, 12, 265–79.

Benton, S.A. et al., 2003, 'Changes in counseling center client problems across 13 years', *Professional Psychology: Research and Practice*, 34, 66–72.

Bifulco, A. et al., 1998, *Wednesday's Child: Research into women's experience of neglect and abuse in childhood and adult depression*, London: Routledge.

Bing, M.N., 1999, 'Hypercompetitiveness in academia: Achieving criterion-related validity from item context specificity', *J of Personality Assessment*, 73, 60–99.

Blatt, S.J., 1995, 'The destructiveness of perfectionism', *American Psychologist*, 50, 1003–20.

BLC (Bread for Life Campaign), 1998, *Pressure to be Perfect*, London: Flour Advisory Bureau.

Board, B.J. et al., 2005, 'Disordered personalities at work', *Psychology, Crime and Law*, 11, 17–32.

Bobak, M. et al., 2006, 'Depressive symptoms in urban population samples in Russia, Poland and the Czech Republic', *British J of Psychiatry*, 188, 359–65.

Braun, O.L. et al., 1989, 'Psychological antecedents of conspicuous consumption', *J of Economic Psychology*, 10, 161–87.

Brines, J., 1994, 'Economic dependency, gender and the division of labour at home', *American J of Sociology*, 100, 652–65.

Brown, G. et al., 1978, *Social Origins of Depression*, London: Tavistock.

Bushman, J. et al., 1998, 'Threatened egotism, narcissism, self-esteem and direct and displaced aggression: Does self-love or self-hate lead to violence?', *J of Personality and Social Psychology*, 75(1), 219–29.

Buss, D.M., 1989, 'Sex differences in human mate preferences: Evolutionary hypotheses tested in 37 cultures', *Behavioral and Brain Sciences*, 12, 1–49.

Buss, D.M., 2000, *The Dangerous Passion*, London: Bloomsbury.

Capron, C. et al., 1989, 'Assessment of socio-economic status on IQ in a full cross-fostering study', *Nature*, 340, 552–4.

Carver, C.S. et al., 1998, 'The American dream revisited: Is it what you want or why you want it that matters?', *Psychological Science*, 9, 289–92.

Caspi, A. et al, 2002, 'Role of genotype in the cycle of violence in maltreated children', *Science*, 297, 851–4.

Caspi, A. et al., 2003, 'Influence of life stress on depression: Moderation by a polymorphism in the 5-HTT gene', *Science*, 301, 386–9.

Caspi, A. et al., 2005, 'Moderation of the effect of the adolescent-onset cannabis-use by functional polymorphism in COMT gene', *Biological Psychiatry*, 57, 1117–27.

Chan, R. et al., 2000, 'Dimensions of personality, domains of aspiration and subjective well-being', *Personality and Individual Differences*, 28, 347–54.

Chang, L.C. et al., 2002, 'Materialism as an attempt to cope with uncertainty', *Psychology and Marketing*, 19, 389–406.

Cheung, C. et al., 1996, 'Television viewing and mean world value in Hong Kong's adolescents', *Social Behavior and Personality*, 224, 351–64.

Christoffersen, D. et al., 1995, 'Examining the relationship between Machiavellianism and paranoia', *Psychological Reports*, 76, 67–70.

Cohen, P. et al., 1996, *Life Values and Adolescent Mental Health*, New Jersey: Erlbaum.

Colla, J. et al., 2006, 'Depression and modernisation: A cross-cultural study of women', *Social Psychiatry and Psychiatric Epidemiology*, 41(4), 271–9.

Collishaw, S. et al., 2004, 'Time trends in adolescent mental health', *J of Child Psychology and Psychiatry*, 45, 1350–62.

Crocker, J. et al., 2002, 'Hopes dashed and dreams fulfilled: Contingencies of self-worth admissions to graduate school', *Personality and Social Psychology Bulletin*, 28, 1275–86.

Crocker, J. et al., 2003b, 'When grades determine self-worth: Consequences for contingent self-worth, for male and female engineering and psychology majors', *J of Personality and Social Psychology*, 85, 507–16.

Deci, E.L. et al., 1999, 'A meta-analytic review of experiments examining the effects of extrinsic rewards on intrinsic motivation', *Psychological Bulletin*, 125, 627–88.

De Mause, L., 1974, *The History of Childhood*, London: Souvenir.

Demyttenaere, K. et al., 2004, 'Prevalence, severity, and unmet need for treatment of mental disorders in the World Health Organization World Mental Health Surveys', *Journal of the American Medical Association*, 291, 2581–90.

Diener, E., 2000, 'Subjective well-being: The science of happiness and a proposal for a national index', *American Psychologist*, 55(1), 34–43.

Dornbusch, S.M. et al., 1984, 'Sexual maturation, social class, and the desire to be thin among adolescent females', *Developmental Pediatrics*, 5, 308–14.

Dunford, B. et al., 2005, 'Out-of-the-money: The impact of underwater stock options on executive job search', *Personnel Psychology*, 58(1), 67–101.

Dunning, D. et al., 2004, 'Flawed self-assessment: Implications for health, education, and the workplace', *Psychological science in the Public Interest*, 5(3), 69–106.

Eagly, A.H. et al., 1999, 'The origins of sex differences in human behavior: Evolved dispositions versus social roles', *American Psychologist*, 54, 408–23.

Eaton, W., 1980, 'A formal theory of selection for schizophrenia', *American J of Sociology*, 86, 149–58.

Eckersley, R. et al., 2002, 'Cultural correlates of youth suicide', *Social Science and Medicine*, 55, 1891–904.

Egeland, J.A. et al., 1983, 'Amish study, I: Affective disorders among the Amish, 1976–1980', *American J of Psychiatry*, 140, 56–61.

Einhorn, B., 1993, *Cinderella Goes to Market*, New York: Verso.

Elder, G.H., 1974, *Children of the Great Depression*, Chicago University Press.

Eley, T.C. et al., 2004, 'Gene-environment interaction analysis of serotonin system markers with adolescent depression', *Molecular Psychiatry*, 9, 1–8.

Emmons, R.A., 1987, 'Narcissism: Theory and measurement', *J of Personality and Social Psychology*, 52(1), 11–17.

European Commission, 2004, *The State of Mental Health in the European Union*, (n.p.) European Commission.

Fabrega, H., 1993, 'A cultural analysis of human behavioural breakdowns: An approach to the ontology and epistemology of psychiatric phenomena', *Culture, Medicine and Psychiatry*, 17, 99–132.

Fehr, B. et al., 1992, 'The construct of Machavellianism: Twenty years later', in C.D. Spielberger et al. (eds), *Advances in Personality Assessment*, Vol. 9, Hillsdale, NJ: Erlbaum, pp. 77–116.

Fejfar, M.C. et al., 2000, 'Effect of private self-awareness on negative affect and self-referent attribution: A quantitative review', *Personality and Social Psychology Review*, 4, 132–42.

Ferri, E. et al., 2003, *Changing Britain, Changing Lives*, London: Institute of Education.

Ferris, G.R. et al., 2001, 'Interaction of social skill and general mental ability on job performance and salary', *J of Applied Psychology*, 86, 1075–82.

Finn, S. et al., 1988, 'Social isolation and social support as correlates of television viewing motivations', *Communication Research*, 15, 135–58.

Florio, M., 2004, *The Great Divestiture*, Cambridge, MA: MIT Press.

Frey, KS, 1987, 'Coping responses of parents of disabled children', unpublished data.

Fromm, E., 1995, *The Essential Fromm: Life between having and being*, London: Constable.

Fromm, E., 2002, *The Sane Society*, 2nd edn, London: Routledge Classics (1st edn: Routledge, 1955).

Froud, J. et al., 2006, *Financialization and Strategy: Narrative and numbers*, London: Routledge.

Fryers, T. et al., 2004, 'Prevalence of psychiatric disorders in Europe: The potential and reality of metaanalysis', *Social Psychiatry and Psychiatric Epidemiology*, 39, 899–905.

Fryers, T. et al., 2005, 'The distribution of the common mental disorders: Social inequalities in Europe', *Clinical Practice and Epidemiology in Mental Health*, 1: 14.

Galbraith, J., 1970, *The Affluent Society*, London: Penguin.

Ger, G. et al., 1996a, 'Cross-cultural differences in materialism', *J of Economic Psychology*, 17, 55–77.

Ger, G. et al., 1996b, 'I'd like to buy the world a coke: Consumptionscapes of the "Less Affluent World"', *J of Consumer Policy*, 19, 271–304.

Gerbner, G. et al., 1976, 'The scary world of TV's heavy viewer', *Psychology Today*, April, pp. 41–5, 89.

Giacolone, R.A. et al., 1989, *Impression Management in Organizations*, New Jersey: Erlbaum.

Gilbert, P., 1992, *Depression: The evolution of hopelessness*, New Jersey: Erlbaum.

Gillespie, N.A. et al., 2005, 'The relationship between stressful life events, the serotonin transporter (5-HTTLPR) genotype, and major depression', *Psychological Medicine*, 35, 101–11.

Goldberg, M.E. et al., 1978, 'Some unintended consequences of TV advertising to children', *J of Consumer Research*, 5, 22–9.

Goldner, E. et al., 2002, 'Prevalence and incidence studies of schizophrenia disorders', *Canadian J of Psychiatry*, 47, 833–43.

Gottesman, I.I., 1992, *Schizophrenia Genesis: The origins of madness*, New York: Freeman.

Gould, S.J., 1988, *The Urchin in the Storm*, London: Penguin.

Gould, S.J. et al., 1979, 'The spandrels of San Marco and the Panglossian paradigm: A critique of the adaptationist programme', *Proceedings of the Royal Society of London B*, 205, 581–98.

Grabe, H.J. et al., 2005, 'Mental and physical distress is modulated by a polymorphism of the 5-HT transporter gene interacting with social stressors and chronic disease burden', *Molecular Psychiatry*, 10, 220–4.

Groesz, L.M. et al., 2002, 'The effect of experimental presentation of thin media images on body satisfaction: A meta-analytic review', *International J of Eating Disorders*, 31, 1–16.

Grolnick, W.S. et al., 1997, 'Internalization within the family: The self-determination theory perspective', in J.E. Grusec et al. (eds), *Parenting and Children's Internalization of Values: A handbook of contemporary theory*, New York: Wiley, pp. 135–61.

Gutierres, S.E. et al., 1999, 'Beauty, dominance and the mating game: Contrast effects in self-assessment reflect gender differences in mate selection', *Personality and Social Psychology Bulletin*, 26, 1126–34.

Hakim, C., 2000, *Work–Lifestyle Choices in the 21st Century: Preference Theory*, Oxford University Press.

Hamilton, C. et al., 2005, *Affluenza*, Sydney: Allen & Unwin.

Harris, C.R., 2002, 'Sexual and romantic jealousy in heterosexual and homosexual adults', *Psychological Science*, 13, 7–12.

Harrison, G. et al., 1988, 'A prospective study of severe mental disorder in Afro-Caribbean patients', *Psychological Medicine*, 18, 643–57.

Harrison, G. et al., 2001, 'Association between schizophrenia and social inequality', *British J of Psychiatry*, 179, 346–50.

Harvey, D., 2005, *A Brief History of Neoliberalism*, Oxford: OUP.

Hauser, R. et al., 2000, 'Occupation status, education and social mobility in the meritocracy', in K. Arrow et al. (eds), *Meritocracy and Economic Inequality*, Cambridge, MA: Princeton University Press, pp. 179–229.

Heine, S.J. et al., 1999, 'Is there a universal need for positive self-regard?', *Psychological Review*, 106(4), 766–94.

Hennigan, K.M. et al., 1982, 'Impact of the introduction of television on crime in the United States: Empirical findings and theoretical implications', *J of Personality and Social Psychology*, 42, 461–77.

Henrich, J. et al., 2005, '"Economic man" in cross-cultural perspective: Behavioral experiments in 15 small-scale societies', *Behavioral and Brain Science*, 28, 795–855.

Hernandez, B. et al., 1999, 'Association of obesity with physical activity, television programs and other forms of video viewing among children in Mexico City', *International J of Obesity and Related Metabolic Disorders*, 23, 845–54.

Hogan, R. et al., 1994, 'What we know about leadership: Effectiveness and personality', *American Psychologist*, 49, 493–504.

Horrobin, D., 2001, *The Madness of Adam and Eve*, London: Bantam.

Hoyenga, K.B. et al., 1993, *Gender-Related Differences: Origins and Outcomes*, London: Allyn & Bacon.

Hutton, W., 2002, *The World We're In*, London: Abacus.

Ickes, W. et al., 1986, 'Machiavellianism and self-monitoring: As different as "me" and "you"', *Social Cognition*, 4, 58–74.

ILO (International Labour Office), 2004, *Economic Security for a Better World*, Geneva: International Labour Office.

Ingleby, D., 2002, 'Introduction to the second edition', in Fromm (2002), pp. xvii–lv.

Inglehart, R. et al., 1994, 'Economic security and value change', *American Political Science Review*, 88, 336–54.

James, J., 2000, 'Do consumers in developing countries gain or lose from globalization?', *J of Economic Issues*, 34, 537–51.

James, O.W., 1995, *Juvenile Violence in a Winner-Loser Culture: Socio-economic and familial origins of the rise of violence against the person*, London: Free Association Books.

James, O.W., 1998, *Britain on the Couch*, London: Arrow.

James, O.W., 2003, 'They muck you up: Developmental psychopathology as a basis for politics', *The Psychologist*, 16, 296–7.

James, O.W., 2007a, *They F*** You up: How to survive family life*, 2nd edition, London: Bloomsbury.

James, O.W., 2007b, 'Selfish Capitalism and Mental Illness', *The Psychologist*, 20, 426–8.

James, O.W., 2008, *Affluenza – How to be successful and stay sane*, London: Vermilion.

Johnson, T.N. et al., 2002, 'Television viewing and aggressive behavior during adolescence and adulthood', *Science*, 295, 2468–71.

Jorm, A.F. et al., 2005, 'Public beliefs about causes and risk factors for mental disorders', *Social Psychiatry and Psychiatric Epidemiology*, 40, 764–7.

Jost, J.T. et al., 2003, 'Political conservatism as motivated cognition', *Psychological Bulletin*, 129, 339–75.

Judge, T.A. et al., 1994, 'Political influence behavior and career success', *J of Management*, 20, 43–65.

Jungeilges, J. et al., 2002, 'Economic welfare, civil liberty, and suicide: An empirical investigation', *J of Socio-Economics*, 31, 215–31.

Kapur, A. et al., 2006, 'Revisiting plutonomy: The rich getting richer', internal report, Citigroup Global Markets, 5 March.

Kasser, T., 2002, *The High Price of Materialism*, London: MIT Press.

Kasser, T. et al., 1993, 'A dark side of the American dream: Correlates of financial success as a central life aspiration', *J of Personality and Social Psychology*, 65, 410–22.

Kasser, T. et al., 1995, 'The relations of maternal and social environments to late adolescents' materialistic and prosocial values', *Developmental Psychology*, 31, 907–14.

Kasser, T. et al., 1999, 'Reproductive freedom, educational equality, and females' preference for resource acquisition characteristics in mates', *Psychological Science*, 10(4), 374–7.

Kasser, T. et al., 2000, 'Of wealth and death: Materialism, mortality salience, and consumption behavior', *Psychological Science*, 11(4), 348–51.

Kasser, T. et al., 2001a, 'Be careful of what you wish for: Optimal functioning and the relative attainment of intrinsic and extrinsic goals', in P. Schmuck et al. (eds), *Life Goals and Well-Being: Towards a positive psychology of human striving*, Göttingen: Hogrefe & Huber, pp. 116–31.

Kasser, T. et al., 2001b, 'The dreams of people high and low in materialism', *J of Economic Psychology*, 22, 693–719.

Kasser, T. et al., 2002, 'Early family experiences and adult values: A 26-year, prospective longitudinal study', *Personality and Social Psychology Bulletin*, 28, 826–35.

Kaufman, J. et al., 2004, 'Social support and serotonin transporter gene moderate depression in maltreated children', *Proceedings of the National Academy of sciences USA*, 101, 17316–21.

Keller, J., 2005, 'In genes we trust: The biological component of psychological essentialism and its relationship to mechanisms of motivated social cognition', *J of Personality and Social Psychology*, 88, 686–702.

Kendler, K.S. et al., 2005, 'The interaction of stressful life events and serotonin polymorphism in the prediction of episodes of major depression', *Archives of General Psychiatry*, 62, 529–35.

Keng, K.A. et al., 2000, 'The influence of materialistic inclination on values, life satisfaction and aspirations: An empirical analysis', *Social Indicators Research*, 49, 317–33.

Kenrick, D.T. et al., 1980, 'Contrast effects and judgments of physical attractiveness: When beauty becomes a social problem', *J of Personality and Social Psychology*, 38, 131–40.

Kenrick, D.T. et al., 1989, 'Influence of popular erotica on judgments of strangers and mates', *J of Experimental Social Psychology*, 25, 159–67.

Kenrick, D.T. et al., 1992, 'Age preferences in mates reflect sex differences in human reproductive strategies', *Behavioral and Brain Sciences*, 15, 75–133.

Kenrick, D.T. et al., 1993, 'Effects of physical attractiveness on affect and perceptual judgments: When social comparison overrides social reinforcement', *Personality and Social Psychology Bulletin*, 19, 195–9.

Kenrick, D.T. et al., 1994, 'Evolution and social cognition: Contrast effects as a function of sex, dominance, and physical attractiveness', *Personality and Social Psychology Bulletin*, 20, 210–17.

Kernis, M.H. et al., 1993, 'There's more to self-esteem than whether it is high or low: The importance of stability of self-esteem', *J of Personality and Social Psychology*, 65, 1190–204.

Kernis, M.H. et al., 2000, 'Master of one's psychological domain? Not likely if one's self-esteem is unstable', *Personality and Social Psychology Bulletin*, 26, 1297–1305.

Khanna, S. et al., 2001, 'Materialism, objectification and alienation from a cross-cultural perspective', unpublished study, cited in Kasser (2002).

Kilduff, M. et al., 1994, 'Do chameleons get ahead? The effects of self-monitoring on managerial careers', *Academy of Management J*, 37, 1047–60.

Kleinman, A., 1988, *Rethinking Psychiatry: From cultural category to personal experience*, New York: Free Press.

Kleinman, A. et al., 1997, 'Psychiatry's global challenge: An evolving crisis in the developing world signals the need for a better understanding of the links between culture and mental disorders', *Scientific American*, 276(3), 86–9.

Krebs, D. et al., 1975, 'Physical attractiveness, social relations, and personality style', *J of Personality and Social Psychology*, 31, 245–53.

Landau, M.J. et al., 2004, 'Deliver us from Evil', *Personality and Social Psychology Bulletin,* 30, 1136–50.

Lasky-Su, J.A., 2005, 'Meta-analysis of the association between two polymorphisms in the serotonin transporter gene and affective disorders', *American J of Medical Genetics*, 133B, 110–5.

Lehtinen, V. et al., 2003, 'Urban-rural differences in the occurrence of female depressive disorder in Europe: Evidence from the ODIN study', *Social Psychiatry and Psychiatric Epidemiology*, 38, 283–9.

Lemann, N., 1999, *The Big Test: The secret history of the American meritocracy*, New York: Farrar, Straus & Giroux.

Levine, M., 2006, *The Price of Privilege*, New York: Random House.

Lewin, E., 1993, *Lesbian Mothers: Accounts of gender in American culture*, Ithaca, NY: Cornell University Press.

Lewis, G. et al., 1993, 'Another British disease? A recent increase in the prevalence of psychiatric morbidity', *J of Epidemiology and Community Health*, 47, 358–61.

Lin, K.M. et al., 1988, 'Psychopathology and clinical course of schizophrenia: A cross-cultural perspective', *Schizophrenia Bulletin*, 14, 555–67.

Lipset, S.M. et al., 2000, *It Didn't Happen Here: Why socialism failed in the United States*, New York: Norton.

Littlewood, R. et al., 1997, *Aliens and Alienists: Ethnic minorities and psychiatry*, London: Routledge.

Loewenthal, K.M., 1993, 'Levels of well-being and distress in orthodox Jewish men and women', *J of Psychology and Judaism*, 16, 225–33.

Loewenthal, K.M. et al., 1995, 'Gender and depression in Anglo-Jewry', *Psychological Medicine*, 25, 1051–63.

Lucey, H., 1996, 'Transitions to womanhood: Constructions of success and failure for middle and working class young women', paper presented at conference on 'British Youth Research: the New Agenda', Glasgow, 26–28 January.

Luthar, S.S. et al., 1999, 'Contextual factors in substance abuse: A study of suburban and inner-city adolescents', *Development and Psychopathology*, 11, 845–67.

Luthar, S.S. et al., 2002, 'Privileged but pressured? A study of affluent youth', *Child Development*, 73, 1593–610.

Ma, G.S. et al., 2002, 'Effect of television viewing on pediatric obesity', *Biomedical Environmental Science*, 15, 291–7.

McHoskey, J., 1995a, 'Narcissism and Machiavellianism', *Psychological Reports*, 77, 755–9.

McHoskey, J., 1995b, 'Nihilism, Machiavellianism, and acquisitiveness', paper presented at meeting of the SouthEastern Psychological Association, Savannah, GA.

McHoskey, J.W., 1999, 'Machiavellianism, intrinsic versus extrinsic goals, and social interest: A self determination theory analysis', *Motivation and Emotion*, 23, 267–83.

McKenzie, K. et al., 1999, 'Risk factors for psychosis in the UK African-Caribbean population', in D. Bhugra et al. (eds), *Ethnicity: An agenda for mental health*, London: Gaskell, pp. 48–59.

Malka, A. et al., 2003, 'Intrinsic and extrinsic work orientations as moderators of the effect of annual income on subjective well-being: A longitudinal study', *Personality and Social Psychology Bulletin*, 29, 737–46.

Mann, A.H. et al., 1983, 'Screening for abnormal eating attitudes and psychiatric morbidity in an unselected population of 15-year-old schoolgirls', *Psychological Medicine*, 13, 573–80.

Manuck, S.B. et al., 2004, 'Socio-economic status covaries with central nervous system serotonergic responsivity as a function of allelic variation in the serotonin transporter gene-linked polymorphic region', *Psychoneuroendocrinology*, 29, 651–68.

Manuck, S.B. et al., 2005, 'The socio-economic status of communities predicts variation in brain serotonergic responsivity', *Psychological Medicine*, 35, 519–28.

Matthews, K.A. et al., 2000, 'Does socioeconomic status relate to central serotonergic responsivity in healthy adults?', *Psychosomatic Medicine*, 62, 231–7.

Mendlewicz, J. et al., 2004, 'Serotonin transporter 5-HTTLPR polymorphism and affective disorders: no evidence of association in a large European multicenter study', *European J of Human Genetics*, 12, 377–82.

Mezulis, A.H. et al., 2004, 'Is there a universal positivity bias in attributions? A meta-analytic review of individual, developmental, and cultural differences in the self-serving attributional bias', *Psychological Bulletin*, 130(5), 711–47.

Mirowsky, L. et al., 1989, *Social Causes of Psychological Distress*, New York: Aldine de Gruyter.

Mishel, L. et al., 2001, *The State of Working America*, Ithaca, NY: Cornell University Press.

Moncrieff, J., 2006, 'Psychiatric drug promotion and the politics of neoliberalism', *British J of Psychiatry*, 188, 301–2.

Morgan, M., 1984, 'Heavy viewers and perceived quality of life', *Journalism Quarterly*, 740, 499–504.

Mortensen, P. et al., 1999, 'Effects of family history and place and season of birth on the risk of schizophrenia', *New England J of Medicine*, 340, 603–8.

Moskalento, S. et al., 2003, 'Watching your troubles away: Television viewing as a stimulus for subjective self-awareness', *Personality and Social Psychology Bulletin*, 29, 76–85.

Murphy, P.L., 2000, 'The commodified self in consumer culture: A cross-cultural perspective', *J of Social Psychology*, 140, 636–47.

Murray, C., 2000, 'Genetics of the right', *Prospect*, April.

Myers, D., 1987, *Social Psychology*, New York: McGraw-Hill.

Myers, L.B. et al., 2000, 'How optimistic are repressors? The relationship between repressive coping, controllability, self-esteem and comparative optimism for health-related events', *Psychology and Health*, 15, 667–88.

Newson, J. et al., 1976, *Seven Years Old in the Home Environment*, London: Penguin.

Nordlund, J.E., 1978, 'Media interaction', *Communication Research*, 5, 150–75.

Norenzayan, A. et al., 2005, 'Psychological universals: What are they and how can we know?', *Psychological Bulletin*, 131, 763–84.

Offer, A., 2003, *Why Has the Public Sector Grown So Large in Market Societies? The political economy of prudence in the UK, c.1870–2000*, Oxford University Press.

Offer, A., 2006, *The Challenge of Affluence*, Oxford University Press.

Olsen, L.R. et al., 2004, 'Prevalence of major depression and stress indicators in the Danish general population', *Acta Psychiatrica Scandinavica*, 109, 96–103.

Orley, J. et al., 1979, 'Psychiatric disorder in two African villages', *Archives of General Psychiatry*, 44, 832–6.

Ovuga, E. et al., 2005, 'The prevalence of depression in two districts of Uganda', *Social Psychiatry and Psychiatric Epidemiology*, 40, 439–45.

Pandey, J. et al., 1987, 'Effects of Machiavellianism, other-enhancement and power-position on affect, power feeling, and evaluation of the ingratiator', *J of Psychology*, 12, 287–300.

Parker, G. et al., 2005, 'Depression in the Chinese: the impact of acculturation', *Psychological Medicine*, 35, 1475–83.

Paul, A.M., 2004, *The Cult of Personality*, New York: Free Press.

Paykel, E.S. et al., 2000, 'Urban-rural mental health differences in Great Britain: Findings from the National Morbidity Survey', *Psychological Medicine*, 30, 269–80.

Paykel, E.S. et al., 2005, 'Size and burden of depressive disorders in Europe', *European Neuropsychopharmacology*, 15, 411–23.

Pedersen, C.B. et al., 2001, 'Evidence of a dose-response relationship between urbanicity during upbringing and schizophrenia', *Archives of General Psychiatry*, 58, 1039–46.

Pickett, K. et al., 2006, 'Income inequality and the prevalence of mental illness: A preliminary international analysis', *J of Epidemiology and Community Mental Health*, 60, 646–7.

Piketty, T. et al., 2006, 'The evolution of top incomes: A historical and international perspective', NBER Working Paper 11955 (available from <www.nber.org/ papers/w11955>).

Pinker, S., 2003, *The Blank Slate*, London: Penguin.

Plomin, R., 1990, *Nature and Nurture: An introduction to human behavioral genetics*, Pacific Grove: Brooks/Cole.

Power, C. et al., 1992, 'Explaining social class differences in psychological health among young adults: A longitudinal perspective', *Social Psychiatry and Psychiatric Epidemiology*, 27, 284–91.

Preston, J.M. et al., 1994, 'Selective viewing: Cognition, personality and television genres', *British J of Social Psychology*, 33, 273–88.

Primary Review 2007-10-12, Primary Review, 2007, 'Community Soundings: The Primary Review regional witness sessions', Cambridge: Cambridge University Faculty of Education.

Rahtz, D.R. et al., 1988a, 'Elderly life satisfaction and television viewership', in M.J. Houston (ed.), 1988, *Advances in Consumer Research*, vol. 15, Provo, UT: Association for Consumer Research.

Rahtz, D.R. et al., 1988b, 'Elderly life satisfaction and television viewership: replication and extension', in S. Shapiro (ed.), *AMA Winter Educators' Conference – Marketing: A return to the broader dimensions*, Chicago: American Marketing Association, pp. 409–13.

Read, J., 2004, 'Poverty, ethnicity and gender', in J. Read et al. (eds), *Models of Madness*, London: Routledge, pp. 161–94.

Read, J. et al. (eds), 2004a, *Models of Madness*, London: Routledge.

Read J. et al., 2004b, 'Public opinion: Bad things happen and can drive you crazy', in J. Read et al. (eds), *Models of Madness*, London: Routledge, pp. 133–46.

Read, J. et al., 2005, 'Childhood trauma, psychosis and schizophrenia: A literature review with theoretical and clinical implications', *Acta Psychiatrica Scandinavica*, 112, 330–50.

Read, J. et al., 2006, 'Prejudice and schizophrenia: A review of the "mental illness is an illness like any other" approach', *Acta Psychiatrica Scandinavica*, 113, 1–16.

Rhodewalt, F. et al., 1998, 'Narcissism, self-knowledge organization, and emotional reactivity: The effect of daily experiences on self-esteem and affect', *Personality and Social Psychology Bulletin*, 24, 75–87.

Richins, M.L., 1991, 'Social comparison and the idealized images of advertising', *J of Consumer Research*, 18, 71–83.

Richins, M.L., 1992, 'Media images, materialism, and what ought to be: The role of social comparison', in F. Rudmin et al. (eds), *Meaning, Measure, and Morality of Materialism*, Provo, UT: Association for Consumer Research, pp. 202–6.

Richins, M.L., 1995, 'Social comparison, advertising, and consumer discontent', *American Behavioral Scientist*, 38, 593–607.

Rindfleisch, A. et al., 1997, 'Family structure, materialism and compulsive consumption', *J of Consumer Research*, 23, 312–24.

Robins, L.N. et al., 1992, *Psychiatric Disorders in America*, New York: Free Press.

Rutter, M., 2006, 'Is Sure Start an effective preventive intervention?', *Child and Adolescent Mental Health*, 11, 135–41.

Rutter, M. et al., 1995, *Psychosocial Disorders in Young People*, London: Wiley.

Ryan, L. et al., 2001, 'Materialism and its relationship to life satisfaction', *Social Indicators Research*, 55, 185–97.

Ryan, R.M. et al., 1999, 'The American dream in Russia: Extrinsic aspirations and well-being in two cultures', *Personality and Social Psychology Bulletin*, 25, 1509–24.

Ryan, R.M. et al., 2000, 'Self-determination theory and the facilitation of intrinsic motivation, social development, and well-being', *American Psychologist*, 55, 68–78.

Ryckman, R.M. et al., 1994, 'Personality correlates of the Hypercompetitive Attitude Scale: Validity test of Horney's theory of neurosis', *J of Personality Assessment*, 62(1), 84–94.

Saha, S. et al., 2005, 'The systematic review of the prevalence of schizophrenia', *PloS Medicine*, 2(5), 0413–0433.

Satoshi, K. et al., 2000, 'Teaching may be hazardous to your marriage', *Evolution and Human Behavior*, 21, 185–90.

Saunders, S. et al., 2000, 'The construction and validation of a consumer orientation questionnaire (SCOI) designed to measure Fromm's (1955) "Marketing Character" in Australia', *Social Behavior and Personality*, 28(3), 219–40.

Schiff, M. et al., 1982, 'How much do we boost scholastic achievement and IQ scores? A direct answer from a French adoption study', *Cognition*, 12, 165–96.

Schimel, J. et al., 2001, 'Being accepted for who we are: Evidence that social validation of the intrinsic self reduces general defensiveness', *J of Personality and Social Psychology*, 80, 35–52.

Schmitt, D.P., 2003, 'Universal sex differences in the desire for sexual variety: Tests from 52 nations, 6 continents, and 13 islands', *J of Personality and Social Psychology*, 85, 85–104.

Schmitt, D.P., 2005, 'Sociosexuality from Argentina to Zimbabwe: A 48-nation study of sex, culture, and strategies of human mating', *Behavioral and Brain Sciences*, 28, 247–311.

Schmuck, P. et al., 2000, 'Intrinsic and extrinsic goals: Their structure and relationship to well-being in German and US college students', *Social Indicators Research*, 50, 225–41.

Schwartz, S.H. et al., 1995, 'Identifying culture-specifics in the content and structure of values', *J of Cross-Cultural Psychology*, 26, 92–116.

Sharpley, M. et al., 2001, 'Understanding the excess of psychosis among the African-Caribbean population in England', *British J of Psychiatry*, 178 (suppl. 40), s60–s68.

Sheldon, K.M. et al., 1995, 'Coherence and congruence: Two aspects of personality integration', *J of Personality and Social Psychology*, 68, 531–43.

Sheldon, K.M. et al., 2000, 'Prosocial values and group assortation within an *N*-person prisoner's dilemma', *Human Nature*, 11, 387–404.

Sheldon, K.M. et al., 2001a, 'Extrinsic value orientation and dating violence', cited in Kasser (2002).

Sheldon, K.M. et al., 2001b, 'What is satisfying about satisfying events? Testing 10 candidate psychological needs', *J of Personality and Social Psychology*, 80, 325–39.

Sheldon, K.M. et al., 2004a, 'Self-concordance and subjective well-being in four cultures', *J of Cross-Cultural Psychology*, 35(2), 209–23.

Sheldon, K.M. et al., 2004b, 'The independent effects of goal contents and motives on well-being: It's both what you pursue and why you pursue it', *Personality and Social Psychology Bulletin*, 30, 475–86.

Shibley Hyde, J., 2005, 'The gender similarity hypothesis', *American Psychologist*, 60, 581–92.

Sigman, A., 2005, *Remotely Controlled: How television is damaging our lives and what we can do about it*, London: Vermilion.

Silverstein, B. et al., 1986a, 'Social correlates of the thin standard of bodily attractiveness in women', *International J of Eating Disorders*, 5, 145–59.

Silverstein, B. et al., 1986b, 'Possible causes of the thin standard of bodily attractiveness for women', *International J of Eating Disorders*, 5, 907–16.

Silverstein, B. et al., 1988, 'Bingeing, purging, and estimates of parental attitudes regarding female achievement', *Sex Roles*, 19, 723–33.

Silverstein, B. et al., 1990, 'Nontraditional sex role aspirations, gender identity conflict, and disordered eating among college women', *Sex Roles*, 23, 687–95.

Silverstein, B. et al., 1991, 'Gender differences in depression: Historical change', *Acta Psychiatrica Scandinavica*, 84, 327–31.

Simon, G.E. et al., 2002, 'Understanding cross-national differences in depression prevalence', *Psychological Medicine*, 32, 585–94.

Simpson, J.A. et al., 1986, 'The association between romantic love and marriage: Kephart (1967) twice revisited', *Personality and Social Psychology Bulletin*, 12, 363–72.

Sirgy, M.J., 1998, 'Materialism and quality of life', *Social Indicators Research*, 43, 227–60.

Sirgy, M.J. et al., 1998, 'Does television viewership play a role in the perception of quality of life?', *J of Advertising*, 27, 125–42.

Snyder, M. et al., 1986, 'On the nature of self-monitoring: Matters of assessment, matters of validity', *J of Personality and Social Psychology*, 51, 125–39.

Srivastava, A. et al., 2001, 'Money and subjective well-being: It's not the money, it's the motives', *J of Personality and Social Psychology*, 80, 959–71.

Surtees, P.G. et al., 2006, 'Social adversity, the serotonin transporter (5-HTTLPR) and major depressive disorder', *Biological Psychiatry*, 59, 224–9.

Susser, E. et al., 1994, 'Epidemiology of nonaffective acute remitting psychosis vs schizophrenia: Sex and cultural setting', *Archives of General Psychiatry*, 51, 294–301.

Swindle, R. et al., 2000, 'Responses to nervous breakdowns in America over a 40-year period: Mental health policy implications', *American Psychologist*, 55, 740–49.

Taylor, S.E. et al., 1994, 'Positive illusions and well-being revisited: Separating fact from fiction', *Psychological Bulletin*, 116(1), 21–7.

Thomas, C. et al., 1993, 'Psychiatric morbidity and compulsory admission among Afro-Caribbeans and Asians in central Manchester', *British J of Psychiatry*, 163–9.

Timimi, S., 2005, *Naughty Boys*, Basingstoke: Palgrave.

Twenge, J.M., 2000, 'The age of anxiety? Birth cohort change in anxiety and neuroticism', *J of Personality and Social Psychology*, 79, 1007–21.

Twenge, J.M., 2001, 'Changes in women's assertiveness in response to status and roles: A cross-temporal meta-analysis, 1931–1993', *J of Personality and Social Psychology*, 81, 133–45.

Twenge, J.M. et al., 2003, 'Isn't it fun to get the respect that we're going to deserve? Narcissism, social rejection, and aggression', *Personality and Social Psychology Bulletin*, 29, 261–72.

UNICEF, 2007, An Overview of Child Well-Being in Rich Countries', Report Card 7, Innocenti Research Centre: Florence.

Walkerdine, V. et al., 1989, *Democracy in the Kitchen: Regulating mothers and socializing daughters*, London: Virago.

Warner, R., 1985, *Recovery from Schizophrenia*, New York: Routledge.

Weich, S. et al., 2006, 'Rural/non-rural differences in rates of common mental disorders in Britain', *British J of Psychiatry*, 186, 51–7.

Weissman, M.M. et al., 1993, 'Sex differences in rates of depression: Cross-national perspectives', *J of Affective Disorders*, 29, 77–84.

Wenglinsky, H., 1997, *When Money Matters: How educational expenditures improve student performance and how they don't*, Princeton University Press.

West, P. et al., 2003, 'Fifteen, female and stressed: Changing patterns of psychological distress over time', *J of Child Psychology and Psychiatry*, 44(3), 399–411.

WHO (World Health Organization), 1973, *International Pilot Study of Schizophrenia*, Geneva: World Health Organization.

WHO, 2002, 'Health and Health Behaviour Among Young People', WHO Policy Series: Health policy for children and adolescents, Geneva: WHO.

Wilhelm, K. et al., 2006, 'Life events, first depression onset and the serotonin transporter gene', *British J of Psychiatry*, 188, 210–15.

Williams, G.C. et al., 2000, 'Extrinsic life goals and health risk in adolescents', *J of Applied Social Psychology*, 30, 1756–71.

Willis-Owen, S.A. et al., 2005, 'The serotonin transporter length polymorphism, neuroticism and depression: a comprehensive assessment of association', *Biological Psychiatry*, 58, 451–6.

Wolfe, J.L. et al., 1996, 'The poverty of privilege: Therapy with women of the "upper classes"', *Women and Therapy*, 18, 597–611.

Worthington, A.C., 2006, 'Debt as a source of financial stress in Australian households', *International J of Consumer Studies*, 30, 2–15.

Young, M., 1958, *The Rise of the Meritocracy*, London: Penguin.

Zillman, D., 1988, 'Mood management through communication choices', *American Behavioral Scientist*, 31, 327–40.

Zimmerman, F.J. et al., 2005, 'Early cognitive stimulation, emotional support and television watching as predictors of subsequent bullying among grade-school children', *Archives of Pediatric and Adolescent Medicine*, 159, 384–8.

Acknowledgements

As with my previous two books, I am indebted to Jemima Biddulph for her role as content editor of this book, this time done at very short notice and with very little time.

Thanks to Avner Offer for his close reading of an early version of the text and the consequent increase in its rigour.

Thanks to Tim Kasser and Richard Ryan, upon whose work I draw heavily. I am also in intellectual hock to David Harvey, Erich Fromm, Michael Young, JK Galbraith and VJ Nunn, to name but some of the thinkers influencing what lies herein.

At Vermilion, particular gratitude to Fiona MacIntyre for indulging my conviction that there was a need for this book. Thanks also to Miranda West, my editor at Vermilion, for a rapid turnaround of the text. Also to John Woodruff and Clare Hulton for their inputs at earlier stages. Many thanks to

Bernice Davison, the copy-editor, for uncomplainingly sorting out a very messy manuscript at very short notice.

My agent Gillon Aitken has stuck by me through thick and thin as the book gradually evolved out of other literary forms (some thick, some thin). I am tremendously grateful to Clare Alexander at Aitken Alexander for her wisdom and intervention at a critical moment.

Finally, as ever, my wife Clare has had to put up with no end of tiresomeness in order for this to be finished in time: thank you Clare.